COMPILED LAW

OF THE

GRAND LODGE

OF

FREE AND ACCEPTED MASONS

OF THE

STATE OF MICHIGAN,

CONTAINING:

I. THE ANCIENT CHARGES AND CONSTITUTIONS; II. THE CONSTITUTION OF GRAND LODGE; III. THE REGULATIONS OF CHARTERED LODGES; IV. THE G. L. BY-LAWS, RULES OF ORDER, &c.; V. THE PENAL CODE; VI. ACT OF INCORPORATION AND CORPORATE BY-LAWS.

PRICE:---Pamphlet Style, 30 Cts; Bound in Cloth, 45 Cts

KALAMAZOO, MICH.:
IHLING BROTHERS, STEAM BOOK AND JOB PRINTERS.
1874.

ERRATA.

Page 23, Sec. 39—8th line—Strike out "to" and insert *of*.

Page 71, Sec. 6—3d line—Strike out "by" after "require"; also, strike out "of" and insert *by* after "vote."

Page 87—6th line—For "make" read *made*.

Page 90—6th line from bottom of page; for "ke" read *be*.

PREFACE.

The recent and thorough revision, by the M. W. Grand Lodge of Michigan, of the Constitutional and Statutory Law of its Masonic Jurisdiction, makes the following compilation a great convenience, if not a necessity, to all Lodges and Brethren that wish to study its provisions. It has been prepared and published by order of the M. W. Grand Master, Bro. Wm. L. Webber; and is furnished to subscribing Lodges and Brethren at cost.

The first place in the volume—the place of honor—has been assigned to the "Ancient Charges and Regulations," not because they are, in form, binding on us, but because they are universally recognized as the beginning and basis of all the "written law" of the Craft; and also because they embody many of those "Ancient Landmarks" which give "metes and bounds" to the Rules and Regulations of Symbolic Masonry.

The careful and thoughtful Masonic student, that delves in the "rubbish" of this Ancient Law, will find the "Landmark" embedded, not in the surface *debris* of its forms and details, but deep down in the sub-soil of its fundamental principles. For Masonry, like the man who cultivates it, has outgrown the *swaddling clothes* and the *feebleness* of infancy; but, like the man, too, it preserves every original and essential *limb*, and *organ*, and *function;* and, though greatly differing in development and power, the infant and the man are identical. It is also true, that the essential elements of Masonry, like those of a true Mason, are not to be found in drapery, manners and customs, the fashion of which may change, but in its physical, mental and moral attributes which, (except as increased by growth,) are unchangeable, and which, by its inherent vitality and generative power, are propagated from generation to generation. The unchangeable "Landmarks" of Masonry, too, like the attributes of a true Mason, are external and internal —written and unwritten—of which the internal or unwritten are the more important, and are to be learned and observed only in secret; while the external or written, which relate wholly to its organic form and visible functions, are those by which the Legislative, Executive and Judicial powers of the Craft are bound to be governed and guided. These written "Landmarks," are few in number, simple in form, broad in their scope, and relate wholly to the essential externals of Masonry; even the written Law of our Jurisdiction, with all its complexity of detail, is but the varied expression of *one* of these comprehensive principles, which, like a "Corner Stone," determines the bearings and form of the entire structure. This underlying principle of our Masonic law may be thus formulated:

It is the right of the Lodge to make and regulate Masons, subject only to the power of Grand Lodge, limited by Landmarks, to make and regulate Lodges.

Of the *relative* importance of the different departments of our Law, it may be well to say: that, while the *Constitution* and *By-Laws* of Grand Lodge, which declare its organic structure and define its functions, are fundamental and worthy of careful scrutiny and observation, the *Regulations of Chartered Lodges are of vital importance to the Craft:* if carefully studied, thoroughly understood and faithfully observed, they will exert a powerful influence in purifying, elevating and preserving the Masonry of this Grand Jurisdiction. The *Penal Code* is, (as it was intended to be,) but a *summary* of the Law of Masonic Trials. It is simple and elementary in form, that it may be the more easily understood by those who, without experience, find themselves compelled to conduct a trial. It should be borne in mind, however, that this Penal Code is not yet and may never be made, by Grand Lodge, "*the Law*" of Trials in this Grand Jurisdiction; but the principles and general rules, of which it consists, will undoubtedly govern Grand Lodge in hearing and deciding all Appeals that may be brought before it.

No one will presume to say that the Masonic Law of this Grand Jurisdiction, as now revised and compiled, is perfect. Perfection cannot be inscribed on anything of human origin. But the Masons of Michigan may congratulate themselves on the solidity, symmetry and harmony that now characterize, in a high degree, the body of their Law. If, with true Masonic "freedom, fervency and zeal," we study and obey it, we shall, from time to time, be able to eliminate its defects and enhance its merits, until it shall stand, as all Masonic structures should, the unmistakable exponent of "Wisdom, Strength and Beauty."

Fraternally,

FOSTER PRATT,

Grand Secretary.

Kalamazoo, September 18th, A. L. 5874.

THE

CHARGES

OF A

FREE-MASON,

EXTRACTED FROM

The ancient Records of Lodges beyond the Sea, and of those in England, Scotland, and Ireland, for the use of the Lodges in London. To be read at the making of New Brethren, or when the Master shall order it.

THE GENERAL HEADS, VIZ.:

I. Of God and Religion.
II. Of the Civil Magistrate supreme and subordinate.
III. Of Lodges.
IV. Of Masters, Wardens, Fellows, and Apprentices.
V. Of the Management of the Craft in working.
VI. Of Behavior, viz.:
1. In the Lodge while constituted.
2. After the Lodge is over and the Brethren not gone.
3. When Brethren meet without Strangers, but not in a Lodge.
4. In Presence of Strangers not Masons.
5. At Home and in the Neighborhood.
6. Towards a strange Brother.

I. *Concerning God and Religion.*

A Mason is oblig'd, by his Tenure, to obey the moral Law; and if he rightly understands the Art, he will never be a stupid Atheist, nor an irreligious Libertine. But though in ancient Times Masons were charg'd in every Country to be of the Religion of that Country or Nation, whatever it was, yet 'tis now thought more expedient only to oblige them to that Religion in which all Men agree, leaving their particular Opinions to themselves; that is, to be good Men and true, or Men of Honor and Honesty, by whatever Denominations or Persuasions they may be distinguish'd; whereby Masonry becomes the Center of Union, and the Means of conciliating true Friendship among Persons that must have remain'd at a perpetual Distance.

II *Of the Civil Magistrate, supreme and subordinate.*

A Mason is a peaceable Subject to the Civil Powers, wherever he resides or works, and is never to be concern'd in Plots and Conspiracies against the Peace and Welfare of the Nation, nor to behave himself undutifully to inferior Magistrates; for as Masonry hath been always injured by War, Bloodshed, and Confusion, so ancient Kings and Princes have been much dispos'd to encourage the Craftsmen, because of their Peaceableness and Loyalty, whereby they practically answer'd the Cavils of their Adversaries, and promoted the Honor of the Fraternity, who ever flourish'd in Times of Peace. So that if a Brother should be a Rebel against the State, he is not to be countenanc'd in his Rebellion, however he may be pitied as an unhappy Man; and, if convicted of no other Crime, though the Loyal brotherhood must and ought to disown his Rebellion, and give no Umbrage or Ground of political Jealousy to the Government for the time being, they cannot expel him from the Lodge, and his Relation to it remains indefeasible.

III. *Of Lodges.*

A Lodge is a Place where Masons assemble and work: Hence that Assembly, or duly organiz'd Society of Masons, is call'd a Lodge, and every Brother ought to belong to one, and to be subject to its By-Laws and the General Regulations. It is either particular or general, and will be best understood by attending it, and by the Regulations of the General or Grand Lodge hereunto annex'd. In ancient Times, no Master or Fellow could be absent from it, especially when warn'd to appear at it, without incurring a severe Censure, until it appear'd to the Master and Wardens that pure Necessity hinder'd him.

The Persons admitted Members of a Lodge must be good and true Men, free-born, and of mature and discreet Age, no Bondmen, no Women, no immoral or scandalous Men, but of good Report.

IV. *Of Masters, Wardens, Fellows and Apprentices.*

All Preferment among Masons is grounded upon real Worth and personal Merit only; that so the Lords may be well served, the Brethren not put to Shame, nor the Royal Craft despis'd: Therefore no Master or Warden is chosen by Seniority, but for his Merit. It is impossible to describe these things in Writing, and every Brother must attend in his Place, and learn them in a Way peculiar to this Fraternity: Only Candidates may know that no Master should take an Apprentice unless he has sufficient Imployment for him, and unless he be a perfect Youth, having no Maim or Defect in his Body, that may render him uncapable of learning the Art of serving his Master's Lord, and of being made a Brother, and then a Fellow-Craft in due Time, even after he has served such a Term of Years as the Custom of the Country directs; and that he should be descended of honest Parents; that so, when otherwise qualifi'd, he may arrive to the Honor of being the Warden, and then the Master of the Lodge, the Grand Warden, and at length the Grand Master of all the Lodges, according to his Merit.

No Brother can be a Warden until he has pass'd the part of a Fellow-Craft; nor a Master until he has acted as a Warden, nor Grand-Warden until he has been Master of a Lodge, nor Grand-Master unless he has been a Fellow-Craft before his Election, who is also to be nobly born, or a Gentleman of the best Fashion, or some eminent Scholar, or some curious Architect, or other Artist, descended of honest Parents, and who is of singular great Merit in the Opinion of the Lodges. And for the better, and easier, and more honorable Discharge of his Office, the Grand Master has the Power to chuse his own Deputy Grand-Master, who must be then, or must have been formerly, the Master of a particular Lodge, and has the Privilege of acting whatever the Grand-

Master, his Principal, should act, unless the said Principal be present, or interpose his Authority by a Letter.

These Rulers and Governors, supreme and subordinate, of the ancient Lodge, are to be obey'd in their respective Stations by all the Brethren, according to the old Charges and Regulations, with all Humility, Reverence, Love and Alacrity.

V. *Of the Management of the Craft in Working.*

All Masons shall work honestly on working Days, that they may live creditably on holy Days; and the time appointed by the Law of the Land, or confirm'd by Custom, shall be observ'd.

The most expert of the Fellow-Craftsmen shall be chosen or appointed the Master or Overseer of the Lord's Work; who is to be call'd Master by those that work under him. The Craftsmen are to avoid all ill Language, and to call each other by no disobliging Name, but Brother or Fellow; and to behave themselves courteously within and without the Lodge.

The Master, knowing himself to be able of Cunning, shall undertake the Lord's Work as reasonably as possible, and truly dispend his Goods as if they were his own; nor to give more Wages to any Brother or Apprentice than he really may deserve.

Both the Master and the Masons receiving their Wages justly, shall be faithful to the Lord and honestly finish their Work, whether Task or Journey; nor put the Work to Task that hath been accustom'd to Journey.

None shall discover Envy at the Prosperity of a Brother, nor supplant him, or put him out of his Work, if he be capable to finish the same; for no man can finish another's Work so much to the Lord's Profit, unless he be thoroughly acquainted with the Designs and Draughts of him that began it.

When a Fellow-Craftsman is chosen Warden of the Work under the Master, he shall be true both to Master and Fellows, shall carefully oversee the Work in the Master's Absence to the Lord's Profit; and his Brethren shall obey him.

All Masons employ'd shall meekly receive their Wages without Murmuring or Mutiny, and not desert the Master till the Work is finish'd.

A younger Brother shall be instructed in working, to prevent spoiling the Materials for want of Judgment, and for encreasing and continuing of brotherly love.

All the Tools used in working shall be approved by the Grand Lodge.

No Labourer shall be employ'd in the proper Work of Masonry; nor shall Free Masons work with those that are not free, without an urgent Necessity; nor shall they teach Laborers and unaccepted Masons as they should teach a Brother or Fellow.

VI. *Of Behavior.*

1. IN THE LODGE WHILE CONSTITUTED.

You are not to hold private Committees, or separate Conversation without Leave from the Master, nor to talk of any thing impertinent or unseemly, nor interrupt the Master or Wardens, or any Brother speaking to the Master: Nor behave yourself ludicrously or jestingly while the Lodge is engaged in what is serious and solemn; nor use any unbecoming Language upon any Pretense whatsoever; but to pay due Reverence to your Master, Wardens and Fellows, and put them to Worship.

If any Complaint be brought, the Brother found guilty shall stand to the Award and Determination of the Lodge, who are the proper and competent Judges of all such Controversies, (unless you carry it by Appeal to the Grand Lodge) and to whom they ought to be referr'd, unless a Lord's Work be hinder'd the mean while, in which Case a particular Reference may be made; but you must never go to Law about what concerneth Masonry, without an absolute Necessity apparent to the Lodge.

2. BEHAVIOR AFTER THE LODGE IS OVER AND THE BRETHREN NOT GONE.

You may enjoy yourselves with innocent Mirth, treating one another according to Ability, but avoiding all Excess, or forcing any Brother to eat or drink beyond his Inclination, or hindering him from going when his Occasions call him, or doing or saying anything offensive, or that may forbid an easy and free Conversation; for that would blast our Harmony, and defeat our laudable Purposes. Therefore no private Piques or Quarrels must be brought within the Door of the Lodge, far less any Quarrels about Religion, or Nations, or State Policy, we being only, as Masons, of the Catholick Religion above mention'd; we are also of all Nations, Tongues, Kindreds, and Languages, and are resolv'd against all Politics, as what never yet conduc'd to the Welfare of the Lodge, nor ever will. This Charge has been always strictly enjoin'd and observ'd; but especially ever since the Reformation in Britain, or the Dissent and Secession of these Nations from the Communion of Rome.

3. BEHAVIOR WHEN BRETHREN MEET WITHOUT STRANGERS, BUT NOT IN A LODGE FORMED.

You are to salute one another in a courteous Manner, as you will be instructed, calling each other Brother, freely giving mutual Instruction as shall be thought expedient, without being overseen or overheard, and without encroaching upon each other, or derogating from that Respect which is due to any Brother, were he not a Mason: For though all Masons are as Brethren upon the same Level, yet Masonry takes no Honour from a Man that he had before; nay, rather it adds to his Honour, especially if he has deserv'd well of the Brotherhood, who must give Honour to whom it is due, and avoid ill Manners.

4. BEHAVIOR IN PRESENCE OF STRANGERS NOT MASONS.

You shall be cautious in your Words and Carriage, that the most penetrating Stranger shall not be able to discover or find out what is not proper to be intimated, and sometimes you shall divert a Discourse, and manage it prudently for the Honour of the worshipful Fraternity.

5. BEHAVIOR AT HOME, AND IN YOUR NEIGHBORHOOD.

You are to act as becomes a moral and wise Man; particularly not to let your Family, Friends and Neighbors know the Concerns of the Lodge, &c., but wisely to consult your own Honour, and that of the ancient Brotherhood, for Reasons not to be mention'd here. You must also consult your Health, by not continuing together too late, or too long from Home, after Lodge Hours are past; and by avoiding of Gluttony or Drunkenness, that your Families be not neglected or injured, nor you disabled from working.

6. BEHAVIOR TOWARDS A STRANGE BROTHER.

You are cautiously to examine him, in such a Method as Prudence shall direct you, that you may not be impos'd upon by an ignorant, false Pretender, whom you are to reject with Contempt and Derision, and beware of giving him any Hints of Knowledge.

But if you discover him to be a true and genuine Brother, you are to respect him accordingly; and if he is in Want, you must relieve him if you can, or else direct him how he may be reliev'd; you must employ him some Days, or else recommend him to be employ'd. But you are not charged to do beyond your ability, only to prefer a poor Brother, that is a good Man and true, before any other poor People in the same Circumstance.

Finally, All these Charges you are to observe, and also those that shall be communicated to you in another Way; cultivating Brotherly Love, the Foundation and Cape-stone, the Cement and Glory of this Ancient Fraternity, avoiding all wrangling and quarreling, all Slander and Backbiting, nor permitting others to slander any honest Brother, but defending his Character, and doing him all good Offices, as far as is consistent with your Honour and Safety, and no farther. And if any of them do you Injury you must apply to your own or his Lodge; and from thence you may appeal to the Grand Lodge at the Quarterly Communication, and from thence to the annual Grand Lodge, as has been the ancient laudable Conduct of our Forefathers in every Nation; never taking a legal Course but when the Case cannot be otherwise decided, and patiently listening to the honest and friendly Advice of Master and Fellows when they would prevent your going to Law with Strangers, or would excite you to put a speedy Period to all Law-suits, that so you may mind the Affair of Masonry with the more Alacrity and Success; but with respect to Brothers or Fellows at Law, the Master and Brethren should kindly offer their Mediation, which ought to be thankfully submitted to by the contending Brethren; and if that Submission is impracticable, they must, however, carry on their Process, or Law-Suit, without Wrath and Rancor (not in the common way) saying or doing nothing which may hinder Brotherly Love, and good Offices to be renew'd and continu'd; that all may see the benign Influence of Masonry, as all true Masons have done from the Beginning of the World, and will do to the End of Time.

Amen, so mote it be.

GENERAL REGULATIONS.*

Compiled first by Mr. George Payne, Anno 1720, when he was Grand Master, and approv'd by the Grand Lodge on St. John Baptist's Day, Anno 1721, at Stationer's Hall, London; when the most noble Prince John, Duke of Montagu, was unanimously chosen our Grand Master for the Year ensuing; who chose

John Beal, M. D., his Deputy Grand Master;

and {Mr. Josiah Villeneau, Mr. Thomas Morris, Jun.} were chosen by the Lodge Grand Wardens.

And now, by the Command of our said Right Worshipful Grand Master Montagu, the Author of this Book has compar'd them with, and reduc'd them to the ancient Records and immemorial Usages of the Fraternity, and digested them into this new Method with several proper Explications, for the Use of the Lodges in and about Westminster.

The Grand Master or his Deputy hath Authority and Right, not only to be present in any true Lodge, but also to preside wherever he is, with the Master of the Lodge on his Left hand, and to order his Grand-Wardens to attend him, who are not to act in particular Lodges as Wardens, but in his Presence, and at his Command; because there the Grand-Master may command the Wardens of that Lodge, or any other Brethren he pleaseth, to attend and act as his Wardens pro tempore.

II. The Master of a particular Lodge has the Right and Authority of congregating the Members of his Lodge into a

*—or the "Anderson Constitutions"; so called, because written by Bro. Jas Anderson, A. M., the W. M. of the Lodge which was numbered 17 at the time the Grand Lodge was formed.

Chapter at Pleasure, upon any Emergency or Occurrence as well as to appoint the Time and Place of their usual forming: And in case of Sickness, Death, or necessary Absence of the Master, the senior Warden shall act as Master pro tempore, if no Brother is present who has been Master of that Lodge before; for in that Case the absent Master's Authority reverts to the last Master then present; though he cannot act until the said senior Warden has once congregated the Lodge, or in his Absence the junior Warden.

III. The Master of each particular Lodge, or one of the Wardens, or some other Brother by his Order, shall keep a Book containing their By-Laws, the Names of their Members, with a List of all the Lodges in Town, and the usual Times and Places of their forming, and all their Transactions that are proper to be written.

IV. No Lodge shall make more than Five new Brethren at one Time, nor any Man under the Age of Twenty-five, who must be also his own Master; unless by a Dispensation from the Grand Master or his Deputy.

V. No Man can be made or admitted a Member of a particular Lodge, without previous Notice one Month before given to the said Lodge, in order to make due Inquiry into the Reputation and Capacity of the Candidate; unless by the Dispensation aforesaid.

VI. But no Man can be enter'd a Brother in any particular Lodge, or admitted to be a Member thereof, without the unanimous Consent of all the Members of that Lodge then present when the Candidate is propos'd, and their Consent is formally ask'd by the Master; and they are to signify their Consent or Dissent in their own prudent Way, either virtually or in form, but with Unanimity: Nor is this inherent Privilege subject to a Dispensation; because the Members of a particular Lodge are the best Judges of it; and if a fractious Member should be impos'd on them, it might spoil their Harmony, or hinder their Freedom; or even break and disperse the Lodge, which ought to be avoided by all good and true Brethren.

VII. Every new Brother at his making is decently to cloath the Lodge, that is, all the Brethren present, and to deposit something for the Relief of indigent and decay'd Brethren, as the Candidate shall think fit to bestow, over and above the small Allowance stated by the By-Laws of that particular Lodge, which Charity shall be lodg'd with the Master or Wardens, or the Cashier, if the Members think fit to chuse one.

And the Candidate shall also solemnly promise to submit to the Constitutions, the Charges and Regulations, and to such other good Usages as shall be intimated to them in Time and Place convenient.

VIII. No Set or Number of Brethren shall withdraw or separate themselves from the Lodge in which they were made Brethren, or were afterwards admitted Members, unless the Lodge becomes too numerous; nor even then, without a Dispensation from the Grand-Master or his Deputy: and when they are thus separated, they must either immediately join themselves to such other Lodge as they shall like best, with the unanimous Consent of that other Lodge to which they go, (as above regulated) or else they must obtain the Grand-Master's Warrant to join in forming a new Lodge.

If any Set or Number of Masons shall take upon themselves to form a Lodge without the Grand Master's Warrant, the regular Lodges are not to countenance them, nor own them as fair Brethren and duly form'd, nor approve of their Acts and Deeds; but must treat them as Rebels, until they humble themselves, as the Grand-Master shall, in his Prudence, direct, and until he approve of them by his Warrant, which must be signifi'd to the other Lodges, as the Custom is when a new Lodge is to be register'd in the List of Lodges.

IX. But if any Brother so far misbehave himself as to render his Lodge uneasy, he shall be twice duly admonish'd by the Master or Wardens in a form'd Lodge; and if he will not refrain his Imprudence, and obediently submit to the Advice of the Brethren, and reform what gives them Offence, he shall be dealt with according to the By-Laws of that particular Lodge, or else in such a manner as the Quarterly Communication shall in their great prudence think fit; for which a new Regulation may be afterwards made.

X. The Majority of every particular Lodge, when congregated, shall have the Privilege of giving Instructions to their Master and Wardens before the assembling of the Grand Chapter, or

Lodge, at the three Quarterly Communications hereafter mention'd, and of the Annual Grand Lodge too; because their Master and Wardens are their Representatives, and are supposed to speak their Mind.

XI. All particular Lodges are to observe the same Usages as much as possible; in order to which, and for cultivating a good Understanding among Free-Masons, some Members out of every Lodge shall be deputed to visit the other Lodges as often as shall be thought convenient.

XII. The Grand-Lodge consists of, and is form'd by, the Masters and Wardens of all the regular particular Lodges upon Record, with the Grand-Master at their Head, and his Deputy on his Left-hand, and the Grand Wardens in their proper Places; and must have a Quarterly Communication about Michaelmas, Christmas and Lady-Day, in some convenient Place, as the Grand Master shall appoint, where no Brother shall be present, who is not at that time a Member thereof, without a Dispensation; and while he stays, he shall not be allow'd to vote, nor even give his Opinion without Leave of the Grand-Lodge ask'd and given, or unless it be duly ask'd by the said Lodge.

All Matters are to be determin'd in the Grand-Lodge by a Majority of Votes, each Member having one Vote, and the Grand-Master having two Votes, unless the said Lodge leave any particular thing to the Determination of the Grand-Master for the sake of Expedition.

XIII. At the said Quarterly Communication all Matters that concern the Fraternity in general, or particular Lodges, or single Brethren, are quietly, sedately and maturely to be discours'd of and transacted: Apprentices must be admitted Masters and Fellow-Craft only here, unless by a Dispensation. Here also all differences, that cannot be made up and accommodated privately, nor by a particular Lodge, are to be seriously considered and decided: And if any Brother thinks himself aggrieved by the Decision of this Board, he may appeal to the annual Grand-Lodge next ensuing, and leave his Appeal in Writing with the Grand-Master, or his Deputy, or the Grand-Wardens.

Here also the Master or the Wardens of each particular Lodge shall bring and produce a List of such Members as have been made, or even admitted in their particular Lodges since the last Communication of the Grand Lodge: And there shall be a book kept by the Grand-Master, or his Deputy, or rather by some Brother whom the Grand Lodge shall appoint for Secretary, wherein shall be recorded all the Lodges, with their usual Times and Places of forming, and the Names of all the Members of each Lodge; and all the Affairs of the Grand-Lodge that are proper to be written.

They shall also consider of the most prudent and effectual Methods of collecting and disposing of what Money shall be given to, or lodged with them in Charity, towards the Relief only of any true Brother fallen into Poverty or Decay, but of none else: But every particular Lodge shall dispose of their own Charity for poor Brethren, according to their own By-Laws, until it be agreed by all the Lodges (in a new Regulation) to carry in the Charity collected by them to the Grand-Lodge, at the Quarterly or Annual Communication, in order to make a common Stock of it, for the more handsome Relief of poor Brethren.

They shall also appoint a Treasurer, a Brother of good worldly Substance, who shall be a Member of the Grand-Lodge by virtue of his Office, and shall be always present, and have Power to move to the Grand-Lodge anything, especially what concerns his Office. To him shall be committed all Money rais'd for Charity, or for any other Use of the Grand-Lodge, which he shall write down in a Book, with the respective Ends and Uses for which the several Sums are intended; and shall expend or disburse the same by such a certain Order sign'd, as the Grand-Lodge shall afterwards agree to in a new Regulation: But he shall not vote in chusing a Grand-Master or Wardens, though in every other Transaction. As in like manner the Secretary shall be a Member of the Grand Lodge by virtue of his Office, and vote in every thing except in chusing a Grand-Master or Wardens.

The Treasurer and Secretary shall have each a Clerk, who must be a Brother and Fellow-Craft, but never must be a member of the Grand-Lodge, nor speak without being allow'd or desir'd.

The Grand-Master, or his Deputy, shall always command the Treasurer and Secretary, with their Clerks and Books, in order to see how Matters go on, and to know what is expedient to be done upon any emergent Occasion.

Another Brother (who must be a Fellow-Craft) should be appointed to look after the Door of the Grand-Lodge; but shall be no member of it.

But these Offices may be further explain'd by a new Regulation, when the Necessity and Expediency of them may more appear than at present to the Fraternity.

XIV. If at any Grand-Lodge, stated or occasional, quarterly or annual, the Grand-Master and his Deputy should be both absent, then the present Master of a Lodge, that has been the longest a Free-Mason, shall take the Chair, and preside as Grand-Master pro tempore; and shall be vested with all his Power and Honour for the time; provided there is no Brother present that has been Grand-Master formerly, or Deputy Grand-Master; for the last Grand-Master present, or else the last Deputy present, should always of right take place in the Absence of the present Grand-Master and his Deputy.

XV. In the Grand-Lodge none can act as Wardens but the Grand Wardens themselves, if present; and if absent, the Grand Master, or the Person who presides in his Place, shall order private Wardens to act as Grand Wardens pro tempore, whose Places are to be suppli'd by two Fellow-Craft of the same Lodge, call'd forth to act, or sent thither by the particular Master thereof; or if by him omitted, then they shall be call'd by the Grand-Master, that so the Grand-Lodge may be always complete.

XVI. The Grand Wardens, or any others, are first to advise with the Deputy about the Affairs of the Lodge or of the Brethren, and not to apply to the Grand-Master without the Knowledge of the Deputy, unless he refuse his Concurrence in any certain necessary Affair; in which Case, or in case of any Difference between the Deputy and the Grand Wardens, or other Brethren, both Parties are to go by Concert to the Grand-Master who can easily decide the Controversy and make up the Difference by virtue of his great Authority.

The Grand-Master should receive no Intimation of Business concerning Masonry, but from his Deputy first, except in such certain Cases as his Worship can well judge of; for if the Application to the Grand-Master be irregular, he can easily order the Grand-Wardens or any other Brethren thus applying, to wait upon his Deputy, who is to prepare the Business speedily, and to lay it orderly before his Worship.

XVII. No Grand-Master, Deputy Grand-Master, Grand-Wardens, Treasurer, Secretary, or whoever acts for them, or in their stead pro tempore, can at the same time be the Master or Warden of a particular Lodge; but as soon as any of them has honorably discharg'd his Grand Office, he returns to that post or station in his particular Lodge, from which he was call'd to officiate above.

XVIII. If the Deputy Grand-Master be sick, or necessarily absent, the Grand-Master may chuse any Fellow-Craft he pleases to be his Deputy pro tempore: But he that is chosen Deputy at the Grand-Lodge, and the Grand-Wardens too, cannot be discharged without the Cause fairly appear to the Majority of the Grand-Lodge; and the Grand-Master, if he is uneasy, may call a Grand-Lodge on purpose to lay the Case before them, and to have their Advice and Concurrence: In which case the Majority of the Grand-Lodge, if they cannot reconcile the Master and his Deputy or his Wardens, are to concur in allowing the Master to discharge his said Deputy or his said Wardens, and to chuse another Deputy immediately; and the said Grand Lodge shall chuse other Wardens in that Case, that Harmony and Peace may be preserved.

XIX. If the Grand Master should abuse his Power, and render himself unworthy of the Obedience and Subjection of the Lodges, he shall be treated in a way and manner to be agreed upon in a new Regulation; because hitherto the ancient Fraternity have had no occasion for it, their former Grand Masters having all behaved themselves worthy of that honorable Office.

XX. The Grand-Master with his Deputy and Wardens, shall (at least once) go round and visit all the Lodges about Town during his Mastership.

XXI. If the Grand-Master die during his Mastership, or by Sickness, or by being beyond Sea, or any other way should be render'd uncapable of discharging his Office, the Deputy, or in his Absence, the Senior Grand-Warden, or in his Absence the Junior, or in his Absence any three present Masters of Lodges, shall join to congregate the Grand Lodge immediately, to advise together upon that Emergency, and to send two of their Number to invite the last Grand-Master to resume his Office, which now in course reverts to him; or if he refuse, then the next last, and so backward: But if no former Grand-Master can be found, then the Deputy shall act as Principal, until another is chosen; or if there be no Deputy, then the oldest Master.

XXII. The Brethren of all the Lodges in and about London and Westminster, shall meet at an Annual Communication and Feast, in some convenient place, on St. John Baptist's Day, or else on St. John Evangelist's Day, as the Grand-Lodge shall think fit by a new Regulation, having of late Years met on St. John Baptist's Day: Provided,

The majority of the Masters and Wardens, with the Grand-Master, his Deputy and Wardens, agree at their Quarterly Communication, three months before, that there shall be a Feast, and a General Communication of all the Brethren: For if either the Grand-Master, or the Majority of the particular Masters, are against it, it must be dropt for that Time.

But whether there shall be a Feast for all the Brethren, or not, yet the Grand-Lodge must meet in some convenient Place annually on St. John's Day; or if it be Sunday, then on the next Day, in order to chuse every Year a new Grand-Master, Deputy and Warden.

XXIII. If it be thought expedient, and the Grand-Master, with the Majority of the Masters and Wardens, agree to hold a Grand Feast according to the ancient laudable Custom of Masons, then the Grand Wardens shall have the care of preparing the Tickets, seal'd with the Grand Master's Seal, of disposing of the Tickets, of receiving the Money for the Tickets, of buying the Materials of the Feast, of finding out a proper and convenient Place to feast in; and of every other thing that concerns the Entertainment.

But that the Work may not be too burthensome to the two Grand-Wardens, and that all Matters may be expeditiously and safely managed, the Grand-Master or his Deputy shall have power to nominate and appoint a certain Number of Stewards, as his Worship shall think fit, to act in concert with the two Grand-Wardens; all things relating to the Feast being decided among them by a Majority of Voices; except the Grand-Master or his Deputy interpose by a particular Direction or Appointment.

XXIV. The Wardens and Stewards shall, in due time, wait upon the Grand-Master or his Deputy for Directions and Orders about the Premises; but if his Worship and his Deputy are sick, or necessarily absent, they shall call together the Masters and Wardens of Lodges to meet on purpose for their Advice and Orders; or else they may take the Matter wholly upon themselves and do the best they can.

The Grand-Wardens and the Stewards are to account for all the Money they receive, or expend, to the Grand-Lodge, after Dinner, or when the Grand-Lodge shall think fit to receive their Accounts.

If the Grand-Master pleases, he may in due time summon all the Masters and Wardens of Lodges to consult with them about ordering the Grand-Feast, and about any Emergency or accidental thing relating thereunto, that may require Advice; or else to take it upon himself altogether.

XXV. The Masters of Lodges shall each appoint one experienc'd and discreet Fellow-Craft of his Lodge, to compose a Committee, consisting of one from every Lodge, who shall meet to receive, in a convenient Apartment, every Person that brings a Ticket, and shall have Power to discourse him, if they think fit, in order to admit him or debar him, as they shall see cause: Provided they send no Man away before they have acquainted all the Brethren within Doors with the Reasons thereof, to avoid Mistakes; that so no true Brother may be debarr'd, nor a false Brother, or mere Pretender, admitted. This Committee must meet very early on St. John's Day at the Place, even before any Persons come with Tickets.

XXVI. The Grand-Master shall appoint two or more trusty Brethren to be Porters or Door-keepers, who are also to be early at the place, for some good Reasons; and who are to be at the Command of the Committee.

XXVII. The Grand-Wardens, or the Stewards, shall appoint before hand such a Number of Brethren to serve at Table as they think fit and proper for that Work; and they may advise with the Masters and Wardens of Lodges about the most proper Persons, if they please, or may take in such by their Recommendation; for none are to serve that Day but free and accepted Masons, that the Communication may be free and harmonious.

XXVIII. All the Members of the Grand-Lodge must be at the Place long before Dinner, with the Grand-Master or his Deputy at their Head, who shall retire and form themselves. And this is done in order,

1. To receive any Appeals duly lodg'd, as above regulated, that the appellant may be heard, and the Affair may be amicably decided before Dinner, if possible; but if it cannot, it must be delay'd till after the new Grand-Master is elected; and if it cannot be decided after dinner, it may be delay'd, and referr'd to a particular Committee, that shall quietly adjust it, and make Report to the next Quarterly Communication, that Brotherly-Love may be preserv'd.

2. To prevent any Difference or Disgust which may be feared to arise that Day; that no Interruption may be given to the Harmony and Pleasure of the Grand-Feast.

3. To consult about whatever concerns the Decency and Decorum of the Grand-Assembly, and to prevent all Indecency and ill Manners, the Assembly being promiscuous.

4. To receive and consider of any good Motion, or any momentous and important Affair, that shall be brought from the particular Lodges, by their Representatives, the several Masters and Wardens.

XXIX. After these things are discuss'd, the Grand-Master and his Deputy, the Grand Wardens, or the Stewards, the Secretary, the Treasurer, the Clerks, and every other Person shall withdraw, and leave the Masters and Wardens of the particular Lodges alone, in order to consult amicably about electing a new Grand-Master, or continuing the present, if they have not done it the Day before; and if they are unanimous for continuing the present Grand-Master, his Worship shall be call'd in, and humbly desir'd to do the Fraternity the Honour of ruling them for the Year ensuing: And after Dinner it will be known whether he accepts of it or not: For it should not be discover'd but by the Election itself.

XXX. Then the Masters and Wardens and all the Brethren, may converse promiscuously, or as they please to sort together, until the Dinner is coming in, when every Brother takes his Seat at the Table.

XXXI. Some time after Dinner the Grand-Lodge is form'd, not in Retirement, but in the Presence of all the Brethren, who yet are not Members of it, and must not therefore speak until they are desir'd and allow'd.

XXXII. If the Grand-Master of last Year has consented with the Masters and Wardens in private, before Dinner, to continue for the Year ensuing; then one of the Grand-Lodge, deputed for that Purpose, shall represent to all the Brethren his Worship's good Government, &c. And turning to him, shall, in the Name of the Grand Lodge, humbly request him to do the Fraternity the great Honor (if nobly born, if not) the great Kindness of continuing to be their Grand-Master for the Year ensuing. And his Worship declaring his consent by a Bow or a Speech, as he pleases, the said deputed Member of the Grand-Lodge shall proclaim him Grand Master, and all the Members of the Lodge shall salute him in due Form. And all the Brethren shall for a few Minutes have leave to declare their Satisfaction, Pleasure, and Congratulation.

XXXIII. But if either the Masters and Wardens have not in private, this day before Dinner, nor the Day before, desir'd the last Grand Master to continue in the Mastership another Year; or if he, when desir'd, has not consented: Then,

The last Grand Master shall nominate his Successor for the year ensuing, who, if unanimously approv'd by the Grand-Lodge, and if there present, shall be proclaim'd, saluted, and congratulated the new Grand Master as above hinted, and immediately install'd by the last Grand Master, according to Usage.

XXXIV. But if that Nomination is not unanimously approv'd, the new Grand Master shall be chosen immediately by Ballot, every Master and Warden writing his Man's Name, and the last Grand Master writing his Man's Name too; and the Man, whose Name the last Grand Master shall first take out, casually or by chance, shall be Grand Master for the Year ensuing; and if present, he shall be proclaim'd, saluted, and congratulated, as above hinted, and forthwith install'd by the last Grand-Master, according to Usage.

XXXV. The last Grand-Master thus continued, or the New Grand-Master thus installed, shall next nominate and appoint his Deputy Grand-Master, either the last or a new one, who shall be also declar'd, saluted, and congratulated as above hinted.

The Grand-Master shall also nominate the new Grand-Wardens, and if unanimously approv'd by the Grand-Lodge, shall be declar'd, saluted, and congratulated as above hinted; but if not, they shall be chosen by Ballot, in the same way as the Grand-Master: As the Wardens of private Lodges are also to be chosen by Ballot in each Lodge, if the Members thereof do not agree to their Master's Nomination.

XXXVI. But if the Brother, whom the present Grand-Master shall nominate for his Successor, or whom the Majority of the Grand-Lodge shall happen to chuse by Ballot, is, by Sickness or other necessary Occasion, absent from the Grand-Feast, he cannot be proclaim'd the New Grand-Master, unless the old Grand-Master, or some of the Masters and Wardens of the Grand Lodge can vouch, upon the Honour of a Brother, that the said Person, so nominated or chosen, will readily accept of the said Office; in which case the old Grand-Master shall act as Proxy, and shall nominate the Deputy and Wardens in his Name, and in his Name also receive the usual Honours, Homage, and Congratulation.

XXXVII. Then the Grand-Master shall allow any Brother, Fellow-Craft, or Apprentice to speak, Directing his Discourse to his Worship; or to make any Motion for the good of the Fraternity, which shall be either immediately consider'd and finish'd, or else referr'd to the Consideration of the Grand-Lodge at their next Communication, stated or occasional. When that is over,

XXXVIII. The Grand-Master or his Deputy, or some Brother appointed by him, shall harangue all the Brethren, and give them good Advice: And lastly, after some other Transactions, that cannot be written in any Language, the Brethren may go away or stay longer, as they please.

XXXIX. Every Annual Grand-Lodge has an inherent Power and Authority to make new Regulations, or to alter these, for the real Benefit of this ancient Fraternity: Provided always that the old Land-Marks be carefully preserv'd, and that such Alterations and new Regulations be proposed and agreed to at the third Quarterly Communication preceding the Annual Grand-Feast; and that they be offered also to the Perusal of all the Brethren before Dinner, in writing, even to the youngest Apprentice; the Approbation and Consent of the Majority of all the Brethren present being absolutely necessary to make the same binding and obligatory; which must, after Dinner, and after the new Grand-Master is install'd, be solemnly desir'd; as it was desir'd and obtain'd for these Regulations, when propos'd by the Grand-Lodge, to about 150 Brethren, on St. John Baptist's Day, 1721.

POSTSCRIPT.

Here follows the Manner of constituting a New Lodge as practis'd by his Grace the Duke of Wharton, the present Right Worshipful Grand-Master, according to the ancient Usages of Masons.

A NEW LODGE, for avoiding many Irregularities, should be solemnly constituted by the Grand-Master, with his Deputy and Wardens; or in the Grand-Master's Absence, the Deputy shall act for his Worship, and shall chuse some Master of a Lodge to assist him; or in case the Deputy is absent, the Grand-Master shall call forth some Master of a Lodge to act as Deputy pro tempore.

The Candidates, or the new Master and Wardens, being yet among the Fellow-Craft, the Grand-Master shall ask his Deputy if he has examin'd them, and finds the Candidate Master well skill'd in the noble Science and royal Art, and duly instructed in our Mysteries, &c.

And the Deputy answering in the affirmative, he shall (by the Grand Master's Order) take the Candidate from among his Fellows, and present him to the Grand-Master; saying Right worshipful Grand-Master, the Brethren here desire to be form'd into a new Lodge; and I present this my worthy Brother to be their Master, whom I know to be of good Morals and great Skill, true and trusty, and a Lover of the whole Fraternity, wheresoever dispers'd over the Face of the Earth.

Then the Grand-Master, placing the Candidate on his left Hand, having ask'd and obtain'd the unanimous Consent of all the Brethren, shall say: I constitute and form these good Brethren into a new Lodge, and appoint you the Master of it, not doubting of your Capacity and Care to preserve the Cement of the Lodge, &c., with some other Expressions that are proper and useful on that Occasion, but not proper to be written.

Upon this the Deputy shall rehearse the Charges of a Master, and the Grand-Master shall ask the Candidate, saying, Do you submit to these Charges, as Masters have done in all Ages? And the Candidate signifying his cordial Submission thereunto, the Grand-Master shall, by certain significant Ceremonies and ancient Usages, install him, and present him with the Constitutions, the Lodge-Book, and the Instruments of his Office, not all together, but one after another; and after each of them, the Grand Master, or his Deputy, shall rehearse the short and pithy Charge that is suitable to the thing presented.

After this, the Members of this new Lodge, bowing all together to the Grand Master, shall return his Worship Thanks, and immediately do their Homage to their new Master, and signify their Promise of Subjection and Obedience to him by the usual Congratulation.

The Deputy and the Grand-Wardens, and any other Brethren present that are not members of this new Lodge, shall next con-congratulate the new Master; and he shall return his becoming Acknowledgments to the Grand-Master first, and to the rest in their Order.

Then the Grand-Master desires the new Master to enter immediately upon the Exercise of his Office, in chusing his Wardens: And the new Master calling forth two Fellow-Craft, presents them to the Grand Master for his Approbation, and to the new Lodge for their Consent. And that being granted,

The senior or junior Grand-Warden, or some Brother for him, shall rehearse the Charges of Wardens; and the Candidates being solemnly ask'd by the new Master, shall signify their Submission thereunto.

Upon which the new Master, presenting them with the Instruments of their Office, shall, in due Form, install them in their proper Places; and the Brethren of that new Lodge shall signify their Obedience to the new Wardens by the usual Congratulation.

And this Lodge being thus completely constituted, shall be register'd in the Grand-Master's Book, and by his Order notify'd to the other Lodges.

APPROBATION.

WHEREAS by the Confusions occasion'd in the Saxon, Danish, and Norman Wars, the Records of Masons have been much vitiated, the Free Masons of England twice thought it necessary to correct their Constitutions, Charges, and Regulations; first in the Reign of King Athelstan the Saxon, and long after in the Reign of King Edward IV. the Norman: And Whereas the old Constitutions in England have been much interpolated, mangled and miserably corrupted, not only with false Spelling, but even with many false Facts and gross Errors in History and Chronology, through Length of Time, and the Ignorance of Transcribers, in the dark illiterate Ages, before the Revival of Geometry and ancient Architecture, to the great Offence of all the learned and judicious Brethren, whereby also the Ignorant have been deceiv'd.

And our late Worthy Grand-Master, his Grace the Duke of Montagu, having order'd the Author to peruse, correct, and digest, into a new and better Method, the History, Charges, and Regulations, of the ancient Fraternity; He has accordingly examin'd several Copies from Italy and Scotland, and sundry Parts of England, and from thence, (tho' in many Things erroneous) and from several other ancient Records of Masons, he has drawn forth the above written new Constitutions, with the Charges and General Regulations. And the Author, having submitted the whole to the Perusal and Corrections of the late and present Deputy Grand-Masters, and of other learned Brethren, and also of the Masters and Wardens of particular Lodges at their Quarterly Communication: He did regularly deliver them to the late Grand-Master himself, the said Duke of Montagu, for his Examination, Correction, and Approbation; and His Grace, by the Advice of several Brethren, order'd the same to be handsomely printed for the use of the Lodges, though they were not quite ready for the Press during his Mastership.

Therefore We, the present Grand-Master of the Right Worshipful and most ancient Fraternity of Free and Accepted Masons, the Deputy Grand-Master, the Grand-Wardens, the Masters and Wardens of Particular Lodges (with the Consent of the Brethren and Fellows in and about the Cities of London and Westminster) having also perused this Performance, Do join our laudable Predecessors in our solemn Approbation thereof, as what We believe will fully answer the End proposed; all the valuable Things of the old Records being retain'd, the Errors in History and Chronology corrected, the false Facts and the improper Words omitted, and the whole digested in a new and better Method.

And we ordain That these be receiv'd in every particular Lodge under our Cognizance, as the only Constitutions of Free and Accepted Masons amongst us, to be read at the making of new Brethren, or when the Master shall think fit; and which the new Brethren should peruse before they are made.

PHILIP DUKE OF WHARTON, *Grand-Master.*

J. T. DESAGULIERS, L. L. D. AND F. R. S.
Deputy Grand-Master.

JOSHUA TIMSON,
WILLIAM HAWKINS, } *Grand Wardens.*

And the Masters and Wardens of particular Lodges, viz.:

I. Thomas Morris, sen. Master.
John Bristow
Abraham Abbot } Wardens.

II. Richard Hail Master.
Philip Wolverston
John Doyer } Wardens.

III. John Turner Master.
Anthony Sayer
Edward Cale } Wardens.

IV. Mr. George Payne Master.
Stephen Hall M. D.
Francis Sorell Esq. } Wardens.

V. Mr. Math. Birkhead Master.
Francis Baily
Nicholas Abraham } Wardens.

VI. William Read Master.
John Glover
Robert Cordell } Wardens.

VII. Henry Branson Master.
Henry Lug
John Townshend } Wardens.

VIII. Master.
Jonathan Sisson
John Shipton } Wardens.

IX. George Owen M. D. Master.
Eman Bowen
John Heath } Wardens.

X. Master.
John Lubton
Richard Smith } Wardens.

XI. Francis Earl of Dalkeith Master.
Capt. Andrew Robinson
Col. Thomas Inwood } Wardens.

XII. John Beal M. D. and F. R. S. Master.
Edward Pawlet Esq;
Charles More Esq; } Wardens.

XIII. Thomas Morris jun. Master.
Joseph Ridler
John Clark } Wardens.

XIV. Thomas Robbe Esq; Master.
Thomas Grave
Bray Lane } Wardens.

XV. Mr. John Sheperd Master.
John Senex
John Bucler } Wardens.

XVI. John Georges Esq; Master.
Robert Gray Esq;
Charles Grymes Esq; } Wardens.

XVII. JAMES ANDERSON, A. M.
The Author of this Book. } Master.
Gwinn Vaughan Esq;
Walter Greenwood Esq; } Wardens.

XVIII. Thomas Harbin Master.
William Attley
John Saxon } Wardens.

XIX. Robert Capell Master.
Isaac Mansfield
William Bly } Wardens.

XX. John Gorman Master.
Charles Garey
Edward Morphey } Wardens.

THE

CONSTITUTION, REGULATIONS,

BY-LAWS, PENAL CODE, AND RULES OF ORDER,
THE ACT OF INCORPORATION AND THE
CORPORATE BY-LAWS,

OF THE

GRAND LODGE

OF F. AND A. M

OF THE

STATE OF MICHIGAN.

ADOPTED:
JANUARY 16th, A. D. 1873, A. L. 5873.

THE CONSTITUTION

OF

THE GRAND LODGE OF

Free and Accepted Masons,

OF THE

STATE OF MICHIGAN.

ARTICLE I.

Style and Title of Grand Lodge.

The name and style of this Grand Lodge shall be "THE GRAND LODGE OF FREE AND ACCEPTED MASONS OF THE STATE OF MICHIGAN."

ARTICLE II.

Membership and Quorum.

SECTION 1. The Grand Lodge shall consist of its Grand Officers, of its Past Grand Masters who maintain membership and good standing in a constituent Lodge, and of the Worshipful Masters of its chartered Lodges or their legal representatives, any ten of whom being present, and having the proper authority, may open and close the Grand Lodge; but, at any general communication of the Grand Lodge, the presence of the legal representatives of not less than fifty chartered Lodges shall be necessary to constitute a quorum for the transaction of business.

SEC. 2. Past Masters, of Lodges in this jurisdiction, who are in good standing, and members of Standing Committees, who are not the legal representatives of Lodges, are members of this Grand Lodge, but without the right to vote.

ARTICLE III.

Rank, Title and Qualification of Grand Officers.

SECTION 1. The officers of this Grand Lodge, their rank and style, shall be as follows:

The Most Worshipful Grand Master.
The Right Worshipful Deputy Grand Master.
The Right Worshipful Senior Grand Warden.
The Right Worshipful Junior Grand Warden.
The Right Worshipful Grand Treasurer.
The Right Worshipful Grand Secretary.
The Right Worshipful Grand Lecturer.
The Right Worshipful Grand Chaplain.
The Right Worshipful District Deputy Grand Masters.
The Worshipful Senior Grand Deacon.
The Worshipful Junior Grand Deacon.
The Worshipful Grand Marshal.
Brother Grand Tiler.

SEC. 2. No Grand officer shall perform any duty of the station or place to which he may be elected or appointed until he has been legally installed; and each officer shall retain the powers and perform the duties of his office for one year, or until his successor has been legally elected or appointed and installed.

ARTICLE IV.

Annual and Special Communications.

SECTION 1. The Grand Lodge shall hold at least one regular or annual communication in each year, and at such time and place as may be fixed by its By-Laws.

SEC. 2. Business affecting the general welfare of the jurisdiction shall not be transacted at a special communication, unless one month's previous notice of the proposed business shall have been given to each Lodge in the jurisdiction.

ARTICLE V.

Qualifications for Office.

No one is eligible, in this Grand Lodge, to the office of Grand Master or his Deputy, who has not served, after a legal election and installation, as the Worshipful Master of one of its chartered Lodges; and no one can hold any elective office in the Grand Lodge of a higher corresponding grade than that to which he may have attained in one of its chartered Lodges; and no one shall be eligible to or hold any office in the Grand Lodge who is not a member, in regular standing, of one of its chartered Lodges.

ARTICLE VI.

Mode of Election and Voting.

SECTION 1. On or before the second day of each regular annual communication of the Grand Lodge, after A. D. 1873, there shall be elected, by ballot, a Grand Master, a Deputy Grand Master, a Senior Grand Warden, a Junior Grand Warden, a Grand Treasurer, a Grand Secretary, and a Grand Lecturer. All other Grand officers shall be appointed by the Grand Master elect.

SEC. 2. In all elections, and on all questions before the Grand Lodge on which the yeas and nays may have been ordered, the representative of each chartered Lodge shall be entitled to three votes; each Past Grand Master and each Grand Officer (except the Grand Tiler) to one vote.

SEC. 3. In all elections, and on all questions before the Grand Lodge, the majority of votes shall govern, unless otherwise provided by law.

ARTICLE VII.

Vacancies—How Filled.

SECTION 1. In case of the death, disability, or absence of the Grand Master, his duties shall devolve on the Deputy Grand Master, the Senior Grand Warden, the Junior Grand Warden, or on the Junior Past Grand Master, or on that one of them present and able to serve, who is the highest in rank, according to the order herein named.

Sec. 2. All vacancies in the other offices of the Grand Lodge shall be filled by appointment of the Grand Master or his legal representative.

ARTICLE VIII.

Supremacy of Grand Lodge.

Section 1. This Grand Lodge, subject to this Constitution and the Ancient Landmarks, is the only source of authority in all matters pertaining to Ancient Craft Masonry within the State of Michigan.

Sec. 2. Any and all organizations, associations, or persons within the State of Michigan professing to have any authority, powers, or privileges in Ancient Craft Masonry, not derived from this Grand Lodge, are declared to be clandestine and illegal, and all Masonic intercourse with or recognition of them, or any of them, is prohibited.

ARTICLE IX.

Powers of the Grand Lodge.

Section 1. This Grand Lodge may grant Dispensations and Charters for holding regular Lodges of Free and Accepted Masons, with the right to confer therein the several degrees of Entered Apprentice, Fellow Craft, and Master Mason; and, when deemed expedient, may annul, revoke, or suspend any Dispensation or Charter.

Sec. 2. This Grand Lodge has jurisdiction over all subjects of legislation and administration; it has appellate jurisdiction from the decisions of Worshipful Masters, and from the decisions and acts of Lodges; it has jurisdiction over its members; and its enactments and decisions upon all questions shall conform to the Ancient Landmarks of Freemasonry, and shall be the Supreme Masonic Law of this jurisdiction.

Sec. 3. This Grand Lodge may fix the location and define the limits of every Lodge under its jurisdiction, and settle all controversies that may arise between Lodges, and has the final decision and determination of all matters of controversy or grievance which may be brought up by appeal or otherwise.

SEC. 4. This Grand Lodge may make and adopt general laws and regulations for the government of the several Lodges under its jurisdiction, and at pleasure may alter, amend, or repeal the same.

SEC. 5 This Grand Lodge may supervise the state and condition of its own finances, and adopt such measures in relation thereto as may be deemed necessary.

SEC. 6. This Grand Lodge may reprimand, suspend or expel any member from its own body for a violation of the Constitution, By-Laws and Regulations of the Grand Lodge, or for any other unmasonic conduct; and may suspend or expel any accused person after trial, upon appeal.

SEC. 7. This Grand Lodge shall, at each annual communication, consider and review the reports and doings of its Grand Officers for the past year, as well as those of the several Lodges under its jurisdiction.

ARTICLE X.

Powers of the Grand Master.

The Grand Master has power—

To convene the Grand Lodge in special communication, in case of emergency; and

To preside at all regular and special communications thereof.

During the recess, or when the Grand Lodge is not in session, he has power—

1st—To issue Dispensations and to exercise the executive functions of the Grand Lodge;

2d—To decide all questions of usage, order, and Masonic law;

3d—To convene any Lodge within the jurisdiction, and in person or by deputy, to preside therein, inspect its proceedings, and require its conformity to Masonic rules;

4th—To issue his Dispensation to any regular Lodge to make a Mason or confer any degree without delay;

5th—To suspend the charter of any Lodge when he may deem it expedient;

6th—To command every Grand Officer, and to call on any of them for information, advice and assistance on business relative to the Craft;

7th—In person or by proxy, to constitute Lodges, dedicate Masonic Halls, lay corner-stones of Masonic Halls, public build ings and structures;

8th—To command a Warden, or any member of a Lodge which he may visit, to act as Warden for the time being;

9th—To cause the Ancient Landmarks and Charges to be observed and to do and perform the duties of Ancient Grand Masters, agreeably to the requirements of Masonry and this Grand Lodge.

ARTICLE XI.

Powers and Duties of Other Grand Officers.

The powers and duties of all other officers of the Grand Lodge shall be declared and defined by its By-Laws.

ARTICLE XII.

District Deputies and their Duties.

SECTION 1. Immediately upon the adoption of this Constitution the Grand Master shall divide the State into ten Masonic Districts, having regard to population, Lodges, and convenience; which districts may be changed from year to year, but the number thereof shall not be increased for ten years, and at the annual communication to be held in A. L. 5883, and every ten years thereafter, the retiring Grand Master shall again divide the State into such number of districts as the Grand Lodge may direct.

SEC. 2. At each annual communication of the Grand Lodge, the Grand Master shall appoint one District Deputy Grand Master for each of said districts, who shall be appointed upon the nomination of a majority of the Masters and Representatives of said Districts, and who shall receive a warrant of his appointment signed by the Grand Master and attested by the Grand Secretary under the Seal of the Grand Lodge; and each Deputy so appointed shall be a resident of his district, and shall possess the other qualifications required in Article V. of this Constitution.

SEC. 3. The ordinary duties of the District Deputy Grand Masters shall be such as the Grand Lodge may prescribe; but the performance of other duties, in case of exigency, may be required of them by the Grand Master.

ARTICLE XIII.

Amendments—How Made.

SECTION 1. This Constitution may be altered or amended in the manner following, to-wit:

The proposed amendment shall be submitted, in writing, to the Grand Lodge, at a regular annual communication; and, unless it be seconded by a majority of the Grand Lodge, on a call of the yeas and nays, it shall not receive any further consideration; but if it be so seconded, the proposed amendment shall be entered upon the records, together with the proceedings had thereon, and as soon thereafter as is practicable a copy of it shall be sent, properly certified by the Grand Secretary, to each Lodge in the jurisdiction for approval or rejection by it. The action of each Lodge thereon shall be certified to the Grand Secretary, by its Master and Secretary under the seal of the Lodge; and if it be found at the next succeeding annual communication of the Grand Lodge, that a majority of the Lodges in the jurisdiction have so certified their approval of the proposed amendment, the question, on its final adoption by the Grand Lodge, shall be taken by yeas and nays; and if a majority thereof shall vote in favor of the proposed amendment, it shall be declared, by the Grand Master, a part of this Constitution; and the Grand Lodge shall then, by vote, determine and declare the date on which it shall become operative.

SEC. 2. The Regulations, By-Laws, and Penal Code of this Grand Lodge shall be amended in the manner following:

Each proposed amendment shall be submitted in writing to the Grand Lodge at an annual communication; and if seconded by the representatives of fifty Lodges, it shall be referred to the Committee on Jurisprudence, and shall lie over for one day; and if it be carried by a vote of two-thirds of the Grand Lodge, on a call of the yeas and nays, it shall be declared adopted.

ARTICLE XIV.

When to Take Effect.

This Constitution shall take effect on the first day of July, Anno Domini, one thousand eight hundred and seventy-three; provided: that so much thereof as relates to the election, appointment and installation of the officers of this Grand Lodge, together with Articles XII. and XIV., shall take effect from and after the time of its adoption; and provided, further: that the officers of this Grand Lodge may be elected, appointed and installed at any time previous to the close of this annual communication.

Done in Annual Communication of the Grand Lodge of Free and Accepted Masons of the State of Michigan, at Detroit, on the sixteenth day of January, A. D. one thousand eight hundred and seventy-three; and A. L. 5873.

REGULATIONS

OF THE

GRAND LODGE, F. and A. M.

OF THE

STATE OF MICHIGAN,

FOR THE CONSTITUTION AND GOVERNMENT

OF

CHARTERED LODGES

ARTICLE I.

The Lodge and its Quorum.

Each Lodge shall consist of a Worshipful Master, a Senior Warden, a Junior Warden, a Treasurer, a Secretary, a Senior Deacon, a Junior Deacon, a Tiler, with such other officers as its By-Laws may provide, and of as many members as may be convenient; not less than seven of whom, in addition to the Master or his legal representative, shall constitute a quorum for work or for the transaction of business; but no Lodge shall engage in either work or business unless its Charter and the Great Lights of Masonry be present.

ARTICLE II.

Rights and Obligations of a Lodge.

The Grand Lodge of the State of Michigan hereby declares:

First—That each Lodge, duly chartered and constituted by its authority, is an integral and constituent part of its Supreme Masonic Power, and has certain inherent and corporate rights.

Second—That a Lodge, by virtue of its inherent rights, as defined by Ancient Landmarks and recognized by this Grand Lodge, has the power—

1. To retain its Charter until lawfully surrendered, suspended or revoked;
2. To meet, and to do all the work of Ancient Craft Masonry;
3. To admit members, and to reject any application for membership;
4. To elect and install its officers;
5. To transact its lawful Masonic business;
6. To exercise, subject to appeal, penal jurisdiction over its members and unfinished work; and,
7. To make By-Laws fixing the annual dues of its members; designating the time of its meetings; and for the regulation of its other internal affairs; but all By-Laws of a Lodge, conflicting with the Constitution or Regulations of this Grand Lodge, are null and void.

Third—That the corporate rights of a Lodge are conferred by its Charter, and by virtue thereof it is entitled—

1. To representation in all communications of the Grand Lodge; and,
2. To protection in the lawful exercise of its inherent rights; to the enjoyment of all privileges and immunities, and the exercise of all powers conferred by the Grand Lodge upon any constituent Lodge.

And it is hereby further declared:

That a Lodge, by its acceptance of a Charter, and its officers and members, by their several Masonic obligations, are bound, in all things, to obey this Grand Lodge, and to be governed by its Constitution, Regulations, Laws and Edicts; Provided, always, that the old Landmarks be carefully preserved thereby.

ARTICLE III.

Duties of a Lodge.

It shall be the duty of a Lodge:

1. To observe and preserve the ancient usages of Masonry;
2. To obey the Constitution and Laws of the Grand Lodge;
3. To render the Grand Master or his Deputy all due respect and obedience;

4. To respectfully hear all official communications from the Grand Lodge, the Grand Master, or any officer acting by their authority;

5. To be properly represented at the annual communications of the Grand Lodge;

6. To provide its officers with their proper jewels and clothing, and itself with a suitable seal;

7. To provide for its meetings a safe and suitable Lodge Room;

8. To furnish the several books required by these Regulations for its Treasurer and Secretary;

9. To make to this Grand Lodge, through its Secretary, its annual and all required reports of its work and condition; and,

10. To punctually pay its annual dues to this Grand Lodge.

For a persistent or inexcusable neglect by a Lodge, or its officers, of any of the duties imposed by this section; for any deliberate violation of its obligations to Masonry or to the authority of this Grand Lodge; for its failure for one year or more, to hold any meeting; or for its failure, for two years or more, to make its annual returns, and to pay its annual dues as herein required, the charter thereof may be suspended or revoked.

ARTICLE IV.

Meetings—Regular and Special.

SECTION 1. The meetings of a Lodge shall be regular and special; and no Lodge shall hold more than one regular meeting in each lunar month; Provided, that regulars may be held on the festivals of the Saints John.

SEC. 2. The By-Laws of each Lodge shall provide on what evening of the week its meetings shall be held, and which shall be regular; but the Master, by giving due and timely notice, may call a special meeting at any other time; Provided, that no business shall be transacted at such meetings but that for which it shall have been called; and, Provided further, that no meeting shall be called or held on the first day of the week (or Sunday) except for funerals or charitable purposes.

SEC. 3. Special meetings may be called for work; for lectures and instruction; for the completion of unfinished trials; for charitable purposes; and for funeral or ceremonial observances, and for no other purpose, except when called by Dispensation of the Grand Master.

SEC. 4. Nothing shall be done in a Lodge while open on the first or second degree, except what appertains to the work and lectures of those degrees. All special or general business, of whatever name or nature, shall be had in a Lodge open on the third degree of Masonry and at a regular meeting, except as provided in the preceding section.

ARTICLE V.

Election and Installation of Officers.

SECTION 1. Each Lodge, at its regular communication next preceding the festival of St. John the Baptist in each year, shall elect, by ballot and by a majority of votes, a Master, a Senior Warden, a Junior Warden, a Treasurer, and a Secretary; and at the same time all other officers required or permitted by Art. I. of these Regulations shall be elected by ballot or appointed by its Master elect, as the By-Laws of each Lodge may direct; Provided; that no brother shall hold more than one office in the Lodge; and that no brother, except a Tiler, shall hold office in more than one Lodge. On the same evening, or as soon thereafter as may be practicable, all officers shall be duly installed by a Present or Past Master, or by the Grand Master or his Deputy, and no officer shall perform any duty of the office to which he may be elected or appointed until he has been so installed; and they shall hold their respective offices until their successors shall have been duly elected, or appointed, and installed; Provided, that no elective officer shall be installed by proxy.

SEC. 2. Except as provided in Sec. 37 of Grand Lodge By-Laws, no one shall be eligible to the office of Master who has not been elected and installed as Warden of a Chartered Lodge; but any one qualified to vote in the election of officers shall be eligible to any other office in the Lodge; Provided, that the Tiler may be a member of another Lodge.

SEC. 3. All members in good standing shall be entitled to vote at all elections.

SEC. 4. If any Lodge shall fail, from good cause, to elect its officers at the time required by Sec. 1 of this article, the Grand

Master, in the exercise of his discretion, may grant the said Lodge a dispensation to hold its election at another time. And in case a vacancy shall occur, from any cause or at any time, in the offices of Master or Warden of a Lodge, upon satisfactory proof of the necessity thereof, the Grand Master may grant his Dispensation for an election to fill such vacancy. But in either of these cases, his Dispensation shall be granted only upon an application of the Lodge setting forth the reasons therefor, to be approved by two-thirds of the members present at a regular meeting, and to be so certified by the Secretary; and of any special election, which may be so ordered in any Lodge, the members thereof shall have due and timely notice.

SEC. 5. Vacancies in the other offices of a Lodge may be filled at any regular meeting, by election or by appointment, as the By-Laws of the Lodge may require.

ARTICLE VI.

The Master—His Powers and Duties.

SECTION 1. The Master shall have power—

To congregate his Lodge whenever he shall deem it proper;

To issue, or cause to be issued, all notices and summonses which may be required;

To discharge all the executive functions of his Lodge; and,

To perform all such other acts, by ancient usage proper to his office, as shall not be in contravention of any provision of the Constitution or Regulations of this Grand Lodge.

SEC. 2. It shall be his duty—

To preside at all meetings of his Lodge;

To confer all degrees in strict accordance with the Ritual ordained by this Grand Lodge;

To give, in full, the lectures appertaining to each degree, at the time it is conferred, in accordance with such Ritual;

To superintend the official acts of all the officers of his Lodge, and see that their respective duties are properly performed; and,

To carefully guard against any infraction, by the members of his Lodge, of its own By-Laws, of the Constitution and Regulations of this Grand Lodge, or of the general regulations of Masonry.

SEC. 3. From the decisions of the Master there shall be no appeal to the Lodge; but appeals from his decisions and complaints of his acts and conduct may be made to the Grand Master or to this Grand Lodge.

SEC. 4. In all cases of a tie vote, except votes by ballot, the Master, in addition to his proper vote, may have the casting vote.

SEC. 5. For any unmasonic conduct, or for the neglect or violation of any duty imposed by the Constitution or Regulations of this Grand Lodge upon the Master of a Lodge, he shall be subject to removal from office, suspension or expulsion.

ARTICLE VII.

Wardens—Their Powers and Duties.

SECTION 1. It shall be the duty of the Wardens to assist the Master in the performance of his duties, and to discharge all others which ancient usage has assigned to their respective stations.

SEC. 2. In the absence of the Master, his duties devolve on the Senior Warden; and if the Master and Senior Warden both be absent, the Junior Warden succeeds to the duties of the Master.

ARTICLE VIII.

Masters and Wardens—Their Reciprocal and Common Duties.

SECTION 1. The Master cannot deputize or authorize any one to open the Lodge in his absence, and to conduct its labors, to the exclusion of a regular Warden present.

SEC. 2. Neither Warden can call a special meeting of the Lodge while his official superior is within the territorial jurisdiction thereof and able to authorize a call.

SEC. 3. The presiding officer of a Lodge, whether Master or Warden, shall not invite any visiting brother to *preside* over his Lodge or to confer degrees, unless he be a Present or Past Master of this or of some corresponding Grand Jurisdiction; but the Master or either Warden present, and presiding over his Lodge, may invite the assistance of any competent brother in conferring the degrees or in giving the lectures.

SEC. 4. In the absence of the Master and both Wardens, the Lodge cannot be opened, unless by Dispensation of the Grand Master.

ARTICLE IX.

The Treasurer and his Duties.

It shall be the duty of the Treasurer—

To receive and safely keep all money or property of every kind which shall be placed in his hands by the Secretary, or by order of the Lodge, and to give proper receipts therefor;

To disburse or transfer the same, or any part thereof, upon the order of the Master, duly attested by the Secretary;

To keep a book or books which shall contain a correct statement of his receipts and disbursements on account of the Lodge;

To make to the Lodge, as its By-Laws may require, annual or quarterly reports of its receipts, disbursements and financial condition; and

To perform such other duties, appertaining to his office, as the By-Laws may require or the Lodge, at any time, may direct.

ARTICLE X.

The Secretary and his Duties.

SECTION 1. It shall be the duty of the Secretary, under the direction of the Master—

To record all the proceedings of the Lodge proper to be written, including its current receipts and disbursements, and all financial reports; and to submit such record to the Lodge at its next regular meeting for approval or correction, and to the Master for his signature;

To prepare and to transmit a copy of such record, or any part thereof, to the Grand Lodge, when required;

To collect and receive all money due the Lodge, giving his receipt therefor, and to pay the same promptly to the Treasurer, taking his receipt for the same;

To make to the Lodge annually or otherwise, as its By-Laws may direct, a report of its work, of the condition of its accounts with its officers and members, and of all other matters relating to its finances or business which may be under his charge;

To keep the seal of the Lodge and to affix the same, with his attestation, to all papers issued under its authority or in obedience to the requirements of the Constitution and Regulations of this Grand Lodge;

To transmit to the Grand Secretary, immediately after each election and installation in the Lodge, a certificate thereof, in the manner and form prescribed by the Grand Lodge;

To transmit to the Grand Secretary the annual return of the work and condition of the Lodge, required in Sec. 40 of Grand Lodge By-Laws;

To report promptly to all contiguous Lodges the name of each person rejected, expelled, suspended, or restored by his Lodge in the manner and form prescribed by this Grand Lodge.

SEC. 2. He shall keep the following books of the Lodge, in such forms as may be provided:

A Roll of Membership for the signature of its members in the order of their admission;

A Ledger, in which he shall record, on pages alphabetically indexed, the names of all belonging to the Lodge; the dates of their initiation, passing, raising, or affiliation; the name number, and location of the Lodges of which those affiliated were last members; the age and occupation of each when received; the dates of their withdrawal, expulsion, suspension, restoration, or death, and their individual accounts with the Lodge;

A Black Book, in which he shall record, upon pages alphabetically arranged, the names of all candidates rejected by his own Lodge, and in like manner the names of those rejected, expelled or suspended by other Lodges, so far as he shall receive the proper notice thereof; and,

A Register, to be kept on the Secretary's desk, in which each visitor shall record his name, and the name, number and location of his Lodge.

SEC. 3. He shall preserve the By-Laws of the Lodge, and the Books of Constitutions and Regulations of the Grand Lodge, which may, from time to time, be published, together with all the printed proceedings thereof, as promulgated by its order.

ARTICLE XI.

Other Officers and their Duties.

SECTION 1. The Chaplain, Deacons, Stewards, Tiler and other officers provided or permitted by Art. 1., of these Regulations, shall perform such duties, consonant with the usages of the Craft, and appertaining to their respective offices, as may be required by ancient custom, by the By-Laws of the Lodge, or directed by the Master.

ARTICLE XII.

The Jurisdiction of a Lodge.

SECTION 1. Every Lodge shall have (subject to appeal) personal and territorial jurisdiction, as follows:

1. Personal jurisdiction is that authority which a Lodge *has* over its members, unfinished work, and rejected material whereever residing, because of their personal relations to it.

2. Territorial jurisdiction is that authority which a Lodge *acquires* over Masons and Masonic Material, because of their residence within its geographical limits, which shall include all territory in this Grand Jurisdiction that is nearer to its place of meeting than to that of any other Lodge in the same Grand Jurisdiction, except as may be otherwise specially provided by this Grand Lodge.

3. By its personal jurisdiction a Lodge has penal power over its members (except its Master, and the Grand Master if a member thereof), and over its unfinished work everywhere; but, by its territorial jurisdiction, its penal power over these persons becomes (as to other Lodges) original and exclusive, so long as they reside within its geographical limits.

4. By its personal jurisdiction a Lodge has the exclusive right to complete its work and to accept its rejected material wherever residing; but it may waive this right in favor of another Lodge, within whose territorial jurisdiction such work or material may have acquired a residence.

5. By its personal jurisdiction a Lodge has no exclusive right to any Masonic material, nor any power over the members and unfinished work of another Lodge; but, by its territorial jurisdiction, it acquires an exclusive right to accept or reject all new Masonic material residing within its geographical limits, and

penal power over all Masons who reside, but do not affiliate therein: Provided, that in a town or city where there are two or more Lodges, the territorial jurisdiction over such resident Masons and material shall be concurrent.

ARTICLE XIII.

Qualifications of the Candidate.

SECTION 1. No Lodge shall initiate, pass or raise a candidate who lacks any qualification required of him by ancient usage and by a Master Mason's obligation; neither shall a Lodge confer any degree upon a candidate who is physically incapable of receiving and communicating, Masonically and perfectly, all that is required by the ritual and work of the several degrees.

SEC. 2. No Lodge shall initiate a candidate who is less than twenty-one years of age, and who has not been an actual resident within its territorial jurisdiction during the twelve months last preceding his application.

SEC. 3. No Lodge shall, knowingly, initiate an applicant who has been rejected by another Lodge in this or any other Grand Jurisdiction, until the rejecting Lodge shall have given its unanimous recommendation and consent thereto, by a secret ballot at a regular meeting.

SEC. 4. No Lodge shall complete the work of another Lodge without its recommendation and consent, given by a two-thirds vote at a regular meeting, to be so certified by its proper officers under seal of the Lodge; Provided, that if the Lodge having jurisdiction of the case be suspended or dissolved, the candidate will be required to obtain from the Grand Secretary of that jurisdiction a proper certificate of his standing.

ARTICLE XIV.

Petitions and Committees.

SECTION 1—

1. Every petition for initiation, degrees, or membership, shall be made in accordance with forms prescribed by these Regulations;

2. It shall be signed by the petitioner, with his name in full,

and be recommended by at least two members of good standing in the Lodge;

3. It shall* be presented to that Lodge in this Grand Jurisdiction, whose location or place of meeting is nearest to the residence of the petitioner; Provided, that a petition for membership from a resident of this State may be presented to any Lodge in this Grand Jurisdiction;

4. It shall be presented at a regular meeting of the Lodge, and shall be accompanied by the fee required by its By-Laws;

5. It shall be referred at the same meeting, to a committee of three to be appointed by the Master;

6. It shall then lie over for consideration, at least one lunar month, and until reported upon by the committee, except as provided by Sec. 9, Art. XV., of these Regulations; and

7. It becomes, when received and referred, the property of the Lodge, and cannot be withdrawn without the unanimous consent of all members present at a regular meeting.

SEC. 2. The committee (if the petition in its charge be for initiation or degrees) shall make strict inquiry and personal examination into the mental, moral and physical qualifications of the petitioner; but in case the petition be for membership, the committee will investigate the moral and Masonic standing of the candidate.

SEC. 3. The report of the committee shall be in accordance with the form prescribed by this Grand Lodge, and shall be signed by not less than a majority thereof; and shall be made at a regular meeting of the Lodge, but not until a lunar month shall have elapsed since the presentation and reference of the petition; Provided, that the Lodge, by vote, may allow the committee further time.

SEC, 4. The report of the committee, when made, shall be read to the Lodge and placed on file.

ARTICLE XV.

The Ballot.

SECTION 1. The right to ballot on conferring degrees or admitting to membership, in a Lodge, belongs only to the members thereof.

---

*See footnote under Article XVII, Section 1,

SEC. 2. The ballot for initiation, advancement, or membership, shall be strictly and inviolably secret; and unless it be *unanimous* in his favor, the candidate is rejected.

SEC. 3. No member of a Lodge shall reveal the color of his ballot, nor question or be questioned thereon; but any Mason who casts a ballot from unworthy or unmasonic motives, violates his obligation; and if he avow any improper motive in his ballot, he is guilty of a Masonic offense, and may be tried and punished for unmasonic conduct.

SEC. 4. The ballot is final, and the candidate is rejected, if two or more black balls be cast; but if only one black ball appear, the Master (before declaring the result) may order a second and final ballot, to be taken at once, to rectify a possible mistake. Whatever the result of any final ballot, the Master shall declare it immediately.

SEC. 5. A ballot shall be had on every petition for initiation or membership reported by a committee to the Lodge.

SEC. 6. No Lodge shall advance a candidate, except by ballot, and after an examination in open Lodge, by which it shall be proved that he has made suitable proficiency in the preceding degree; Provided, that such examination and ballot may be had at any meeting called for work; and, provided further, that the formal application of a candidate for advancement, in a Lodge that conferred the preceding degree, need not be referred to a committee, unless such reference be demanded by a member of the Lodge.

SEC. 7. After a ballot has been ordered, or is in progress, it cannot be suspended or postponed; neither can a ballot be reconsidered.

SEC. 8. Though a candidate may be elected by a unanimous ballot, to receive any degree, if, before it is conferred, the Master is satisfied that he is unworthy, it shall be his duty to refuse to confer the degree; or, if before the degree is conferred, any member of the Lodge *object*, the candidate shall neither be initiated or advanced until the objection is waived or withdrawn. The election of a brother to membership is final; no objection made after election shall change the result.

SEC. 9. No Lodge shall ballot on a petition (except by Dispensation from the Grand Master) until it has laid over not less than one lunar month; and it shall not, in any case, ballot upon a petition until after it has been referred to and reported upon by a committee; neither shall a Lodge ballot on a petition at a special meeting, except by a Dispensation from the Grand Master; and of such special meeting and the purpose thereof, the members of the Lodge shall have due notice.

SEC. 10. Except by Dispensation of the Grand Master, no Lodge shall confer the first or second degree on more than five candidates, nor more than one degree on any candidate at one meeting; neither shall the interval between the initiation and the raising of a candidate be less than one lunar month. The first and second sections of the third degree shall not be conferred on more than one candidate at a time.

ARTICLE XVI.

Membership in a Lodge.

SECTION 1. A man, by initiation, becomes a Mason, and is subject to the laws of Masonry; but he does not thereby become a member of a Lodge.

SEC. 2. When a brother is made a Master Mason, he thereby becomes a member of the Lodge electing him to the degree; Provided, that when a Lodge confers the Master Mason's degree upon a candidate, at the request of another Lodge, his membership shall be with the Lodge requesting the work.

SEC. 3. Membership in a Lodge may be acquired by affiliation; but no Lodge shall act on a petition for membership which is not accompanied by a proper dimit from the Lodge of which the applicant was last a member, except by Dispensation from the Grand Master.

SEC. 4. A brother's dimit or other documentary evidence of his standing in Masonry, is his property until he is elected a member of a Lodge, when it becomes the property of that Lodge and must be cancelled, and carefully preserved among its files; but if his application be rejected, it must be returned to him uncancelled.

SEC. 5. A brother living in this Grand Jurisdiction, is not required to affiliate with the Lodge nearest his residence;

but he may become a member of any Lodge in this State that will receive him.

SEC. 6. No Lodge in this Grand Jurisdiction shall receive a petition from, or admit to membership, a brother whose residence is in another State.

SEC. 7. No Lodge shall admit to full membership a brother who is a member of another Lodge; Provided this shall be no bar to honorary membership.

SEC. 8. The only voluntary termination of membership in a particular Lodge, that can be recognized as Masonic and proper, is by dimit.

SEC. 9. A brother in good standing may apply to his Lodge for a dimit, giving his reasons therefor; if it appear that he is not under charges, and has paid his dues to the Lodge, it may, by a majority vote at a regular meeting, grant his request.

SEC. 10. All dimit certificates issued by Lodges in this Grand Jurisdiction, shall be in the form prescribed by this Grand Lodge, but the vote of the Lodge is *the dimit*, and the certificate thereof shall bear the date of the vote, and the brother's membership in the Lodge shall cease from the same date.

SEC. 11. A brother thus dimitted, who desires to renew his membership in the Lodge upon a dimit granted by it, shall proceed by petition, which shall be referred to a committee, and be otherwise acted on by the Lodge, as in all other cases of unaffiliated Masons.

ARTICLE XVII.

Rejected Candidates.

SECTION 1. A candidate for initiation or advancement, that has been rejected, by a Lodge having jurisdiction, may renew his application to *the same Lodge* at any succeeding regular meeting thereof; but if such applicant change his residence he shall* apply to a Lodge of the jurisdiction in which he resides; but such Lodge shall not confer any degree on such applicant without the recommendation and consent thereto of the Lodge having personal jurisdiction of the material.

*By a decision of Grand Master McCurdy, approved by Grand Lodge, "shall," in this connection, is construed to have the force and meaning of *may*.

SEC. 2. A brother, whose application for membership has been rejected by a Lodge, may renew his application to the same or any other Lodge in this State, as he may elect. The rejection of the petition of a dimitted brother does not affect his Masonic standing.

ARTICLE XVIII.

Fees and Dues.

SECTION 1. No Lodge shall confer the three degrees of Masonry for less than twenty-one dollars; and the By-Laws of each Lodge shall provide how this or a larger amount shall be divided between the degrees; and what shall be the fee, if any, for membership.

SEC. 2. No Lodge shall initiate, pass or raise any candidate, or elect any brother to membership until the proper fee has been received by the Secretary; Provided that the fee accompanying the petition of a rejected applicant shall be returned to him.

SEC. 3. Every Lodge conferring degrees without the usual delay, or at a special meeting, requiring a Dispensation from the Grand Master, shall charge each of such candidates, ten dollars in addition to its regular fees.

SEC. 4. The By-Laws of each Lodge shall fix the sum to be annually paid by each member thereof as his dues to the Lodge.

SEC. 5. A Lodge, by vote at a regular meeting, may remit the dues of a brother unable to pay them.

ARTICLE XIX.

Visitors.

SECTION 1. The right of every affiliated Master Mason, in good standing, to visit a Lodge, is subordinate to the right of the Lodge to receive the visit; and the Master shall not admit any visitor in opposition to a vote of his Lodge, or to the objection of a member thereof.

SEC. 2. No visitor shall be admitted to a Lodge until his Masonic qualifications have been duly ascertained by due trial and strict examination, or by lawful Masonic information; the trial and examination may be made by the Master, or by a competent brother or committee designated by the Master; the result of which, together with the name, Lodge and residence of the visitor shall be reported in open Lodge, before the visitor is introduced.

SEC. 3. A visiting brother has the right to see the charter of the Lodge he is about to visit.

SEC. 4. No voluntarily unaffiliated Mason residing within the territorial jurisdiction of a Lodge shall have the privilege of visiting the same more than three times; and no unaffiliated Mason shall be permitted to visit more than once any Lodge beyond the territorial jurisdiction of which he may be a resident.

ARTICLE XX.

Place of Meeting.

SECTION 1. This Grand Lodge will not change the location of a chartered Lodge without its consent; but no Lodge shall change its place of meeting, so as to affect the territorial jurisdiction of contiguous Lodges, without one month's notice to such Lodges, a two-thirds vote of its own members present at a regular meeting, and the consent thereto of this Grand Lodge.

SEC. 2. A Lodge located in a village or city, by a two-thirds vote of its members present at a regular meeting, and with the consent of the Grand Master, may change its place of meeting from one building to another, within the corporate limits of such village or city; Provided, that notice of such proposed change shall have been given to its members at its last preceding regular meeting.

ARTICLE XXI.

Funerals and Processions.

SECTION 1. No Lodge shall form a public procession for the funeral of a Master Mason, without the permission of its Master or his legal representative, nor for any other purpose without a Dispensation from the Grand Master; and no procession of

Masons shall be permitted on any other than strictly Masonic occasions.

SEC. 2. None but Master Masons shall be permitted to join a Masonic funeral procession.

Done in Annual Communication of the Grand Lodge of Free and Accepted Masons of the State of Michigan, at Detroit, on the sixteenth day of January, A. D. one thousand eight hundred and seventy-three; and A. L. 5873. Ordered to take effect on the first day of July, A. L. 5873.

BY-LAWS

OF THE

GRAND LODGE, F. and A. M.

OF THE

STATE OF MICHIGAN,

Meetings.

SECTION 1. The annual communication of the Grand Lodge shall, unless otherwise ordered, be held in the city of Detroit, on the fourth Tuesday of January, at 12 o'clock, noon.

Order of Business.

SEC. 2. After the opening of the Grand Lodge the order of business shall be as follows, viz.:

1. Reading the Records.
2. Report of the Grand Master.
3. Reports of other Grand Officers.
4. Reports of Standing Committees in their order.
5. Miscellaneous Business.
6. Installation of officers and appointment of Standing Committees.

SEC. 3. This order of business may at any time be suspended or changed by a two-thirds vote.

SEC. 4. At special communications the order of business shall be such as the Grand Master may direct.

Duties of Grand Officers.

SEC. 5. The Deputy Grand Master shall assist the Grand Master as he may direct, and in the case of the death or absence of the Grand Master, shall preside at all meetings of the Grand Lodge, and shall exercise all of the prerogatives and perform all the duties of Grand Master until a successor be chosen.

SEC. 6. The Grand Wardens shall assist the Grand Master in the Grand Lodge as he may direct, ordinarily performing the duties pertaining to their respective offices, and in case of the death or absence of the Grand Master and Deputy Grand Master shall, according to rank, preside at the communications of the Grand Lodge, and exercise all the powers and perform all the duties of Grand Master until a successor be chosen.

SEC. 7. The Grand Treasurer shall have charge of all the funds, property, securities and vouchers of the Grand Lodge, and it shall be his duty to attend at all communications, and, if directed by the Grand Master, to meet the Grand Officers and Committees of the Grand Lodge, with the books and all necessary documents relating to his office; to make a full report at the annual communication; to give bonds for the faithful discharge of his trusts in such sum and with such sureties as shall be approved by the Grand Master and Finance Committee; he shall receive all moneys from the Grand Secretary, shall pay the orders of the Grand Master authorized by the Grand Lodge, and finally, shall pay or deliver over to his successor in office, or such other person or persons as the Grand Lodge may appoint, all the funds, property, securities, vouchers, records and books belonging to the Grand Lodge.

SEC. 8. The Grand Secretary shall attend at all regular and special communications of the Grand Lodge, and duly record its proceedings, and shall receive and accurately account for, and promptly pay or deliver over to the Grand Treasurer all the funds and property of the Grand Lodge, from whatever source, taking his receipt for the same. He shall make a record of the returns made by constituent Lodges; receive and preserve all petitions, applications, appeals, and other documents; sign, certify to, and duly seal all instruments of writing emanating from the Grand Lodge; conduct the correspondence of the Grand Lodge under the direction of the Grand Master; and report annually to the several Grand Lodges in correspondence with this Grand Lodge the names of the Grand Officers elected. He shall at each annual communication make a report to the Grand Lodge of moneys received and paid over to the Grand Treasurer; of failure or want of punctuality on the part of constituent Lodges in paying dues and making proper returns: and of such other matters, as, in his judgment, may require the action of the Grand Lodge. He shall in due time, previous to each annual communication, furnish each Lodge in this jurisdiction with blank returns and with such instructions in regard to them as the regulations and laws of the Grand Lodge may require. He shall give bonds for the faithful discharge of his trusts, and for the prompt delivery to his successor in office of all the books, papers, and other property of the Grand Lodge in such sum, and with such sureties as shall be approved by the Grand Master and the Finance Committee. He shall cause the Transactions of this Grand Lodge to be published annually within forty days of the close of each annual session, and shall publish therewith its Constitution, Regulations, By-Laws, and Standing Resolutions, whenever ordered by the Grand Lodge.

SEC. 9. The Grand Lecturer shall thoroughly acquaint himself with the work and lectures of the three degrees of Ancient Craft Masonry, according to the standard of this Grand Lodge; shall visit the several Lodges in this jurisdiction as extensively as possible, and instruct them in the work, lectures, and ceremonies; he shall report to the Grand Master; in writing, any deviations in the work or lectures from the system of this Grand Lodge; and he shall have charge of teaching it during his term of office, subject always to the Grand Master.

SEC. 10. The Grand Chaplain shall attend the communications of the Grand Lodge and conduct such religious services as are established by the usages of ancient Craft Masonry.

SEC. 11. The District Deputy Grand Masters shall have the general oversight of Lodges within their separate districts, and may exercise the powers of the Grand Master, so far as relates to the convening of Lodges and presiding therein, and, under the direction of the Grand Master, may suspend their functions and may constitute new Lodges. It shall be the special duty of each to examine the work and proceedings of Lodges in his district, and to convene the officers of the different Lodges at such time and place as may be agreed upon by the Grand Lecturer and himself, for the purpose of receiving instruction from the Grand Lecturer.

They shall make reports of their doings quarterly, and oftener if required, to the Grand Master; and appeals to the Grand Master may at all times be taken from their decisions.

For unmasonic conduct, neglect of duty, incompetency, or for other good and sufficient reasons, the Grand Master may, at any time, suspend or revoke the appointment of any District Deputy, and the Grand Master shall report his action in every such case to the Grand Lodge.

SEC. 12. The Senior and Junior Grand Deacons shall perform the duties which by ancient usage pertain to their respective offices.

SEC. 13. The Grand Marshal shall proclaim the Grand Officers at their installation, introduce the representatives of foreign Grand Lodges and distinguished visiting brethren, conduct processions of the Grand Lodge, and communicate and execute all commands of the Grand Master not otherwise provided for.

SEC. 14. The Grand Tiler shall guard the door of the Grand Lodge upon the outside, and perform the duties incident to his office.

SEC. 15. In addition to the officers named in the Constitution of the Grand Lodge, the Grand Master may appoint at the opening of each communication, from its members, a Grand Architect, Grand Standard Bearer, Grand Sword Bearer, Grand Pursuivant, and two Grand Stewards. The title of each shall be Worshipful, and the rank that accorded by Masonic usage. Their terms of office shall expire at the close of the communication for which they were appointed.

SEC. 16. The Grand Standard Bearer shall take charge of the Grand Standard in processions and public ceremonies, and perform such other services as may be required of him by the Grand Master.

SEC. 17. The Grand Sword Bearer shall act as assistant to the Grand Marshal, act as his substitute in his absence, and perform such other duties as by ancient usage pertain to his office.

SEC. 18. The Grand Pursuivant shall be stationed at the inner door of the Grand Lodge, and it shall be his duty to announce all applicants for admission by their Masonic title, name and connection ; to see that they appear in Grand Lodge suitably clothed and, under the direction of the Grand Marshal, that they take their proper stations.

SEC. 19. The Grand Stewards shall perform the duties of their offices in accordance with ancient usage, and shall also have charge of the jewels and clothing of the Grand Lodge during its communications.

Standing Committees and their Duties.

SEC. 20. At each annual communication of the Grand Lodge, immediately after the installation of officers, the Grand Master shall appoint the following Standing Committees, who shall hold their office for one year, or until their successors are appointed, and shall be entitled to the same per-diem and mileage as other officers of the Grand Lodge:

First—On Jurisprudence, to consist of three members, whose duty it shall be to examine and report upon all questions of Masonic Law submitted to them for investigation:

Second—On Appeals, consisting of three members whose duty it shall be to examine and report upon all appeals, memorials, and petitions in relation to any matter of complaint or grievance within this jurisdiction, which shall come before the Grand Lodge:

Third—On Finance, consisting of three members whose duty it shall be to examine the accounts of the Grand Treasurer and Grand Secretary, and all accounts and financial matters to them referred; the mileage and per-diem due to each officer and member of the Grand Lodge; and to make a full report, at each annual communication, of the financial condition of the Grand Lodge:

Fourth—On Lodges, consisting of three members, whose duty it shall be to examine the records of work and the returns of Lodges, under Dispensation; and to make reports to the Grand Lodge if, (or not) in their opinion, charters should be granted to such Lodges; and also to examine and report upon any returns of proceedings of chartered Lodges which may be referred to them:

Fifth—On Credentials, to consist of three members, whose duty it shall be to examine the credentials of all persons claiming the right of membership, and report their names and Masonic connection to the Grand Lodge:

Sixth—On Correspondence, to consist of three members, of

which committee the Grand Secretary shall be chairman, whose duty it shall be to examine the correspondence and reports from other Grand Lodges in correspondence with this Grand Lodge and report at each annual communication whatever may seem of sufficient importance and interest to demand attention or action.

SEC. 21. All of the previous named committees, together with the Grand Master, Grand Treasurer, and Grand Secretary, shall convene at the place of holding the annual communication of the Grand Lodge, at least twenty-four hours previous to its opening, and shall be entitled to the same per-diem as is allowed to members of the Grand Lodge; and any of the above committees may be convened at such time and place as the Grand Master may deem necessary, and, when so convened, shall be entitled to the per-diem and mileage allowed members of the Grand Lodge.

Special Committees.

SEC. 22. Such special committees as may be deemed necessary may be appointed to act at the pleasure of the Grand Lodge.

Compensation of Officers, Committees and Members.

SEC. 23. The Grand Officers and members of this Grand Lodge entitled to vote, shall receive three dollars per-diem for each day's actual attendance upon all annual and special communications, and five cents per mile for each mile traveled in going to and returning from the same—the route and distance to be determined by the Finance Committee—Provided that no representative shall receive either mileage or per-diem, unless the dues to the Grand Lodge, of the Lodge which he represents, shall previously have been paid or remitted. To the foregoing are the following exceptions, viz.:

SEC. 24. The Grand Master shall receive for his expenses five hundred dollars per annum, and the mileage named above for each mile traveled in the performance of his official duties; each District Deputy Grand Master shall receive, for each day spent, and for each mile traveled in the performance of his official duties, the per-diem and mileage allowed to members of Grand Lodge; the Grand Secretary shall receive an annual salary of eight hundred dollars and the mileage allowed other members of the Grand Lodge; the Grand Lecturer shall receive an annual salary of five hundred dollars and the same mileage as is paid members of the Grand Lodge, for each mile traveled in the performance of his official duties, and for attendance upon Schools of Instruction he shall receive an additional compensation of three dollars per day; the compensation named shall be due and payable quarterly, on the first days of April, July, October and January.

SEC. 25. Standing and special committees, when convened pursuant to these By-Laws, shall be entitled to the same mileage and per-diem allowed members of the Grand Lodge.

Grand Lodge Revenues.

SEC. 26. The revenues of this Grand Lodge shall be derived as may be otherwise provided in these By-Laws, and from the following sources, viz.:

First—For every warrant or charter to form a new Lodge, $100.00.

Second—For every Dispensation to form a new Lodge,—to be deducted from fee for charter in case the Lodge shall subsequently be chartered by this Grand Lodge, $50.

Third—All other Dispensations, $5.

Fourth—For every Grand Lodge certificate, $1.00, one-half of which shall belong to the Grand Secretary.

Fifth—All chartered Lodges in this Jurisdiction shall pay annually to the Grand Lodge, before the tenth day of January, for every person initiated, one dollar; for every Master Mason, from without the jurisdiction of this Grand Lodge, admitted to membership, one dollar; and for each Master Mason, who is a member of the Lodge at the close of the Masonic year, (honorary members, suspended members, members whose dues may be remitted on charitable considerations and Secretaries excepted,) twenty-five cents.

SEC. 27. All moneys received by the Grand Secretary for use of Grand Lodge Seal, for certificates, blanks, and other papers authorized by the Grand Lodge or issued by its direction, shall be accounted for to the Grand Lodge and paid to the Grand Treasurer.

Proxies.

SEC. 28. Whenever the Master of a Lodge cannot attend the communication of the Grand Lodge, the Senior or Junior Warden, shall, according to rank, be his proxy, and the legal representative of the Lodge. In case of the failure or inability of either of these to attend, the Lodge may, at its last regular communication in December, elect of its members any Master Mason in good standing, as the Representative of the Lodge, and he shall receive a certificate of his appointment in writing signed by the Master, and under the seal of the Lodge electing him.

Clothing and Jewels.

SEC. 29. The officers and members of this Grand Lodge when convened shall wear the ordinary clothing of the Master Mason, and the officers shall also wear upon their left breast the jewels appropriate to their several offices, which shall be made of gilt or yellow metal. The jewels shall be suspended by purple ribbon, at either end of which shall be a bar, and equally between the bars a slide of the same metal as the jewel. Upon the upper bar shall be inscribed the words "Grand Lodge;" upon the slide the initials "F. & A. M.;" and upon the lower bar the word "Michigan."

Lodges Under Dispensation.

SEC. 30. Lodges under Dispensation may be constituted by the Grand Master or Grand Lodge upon the petition of not less than eight Master Masons in good standing, and in which their Master and Wardens shall be nominated. Said petition shall set forth the name of the village, town, place, or city and county in which the Lodge is to be established; also the proposed name of the Lodge; that the petitioners have procured a suitable room, with convenient ante-rooms, for the practice of Masonic rites; that the material in their proposed jurisdiction is sufficient to sustain a healthy and reputable Lodge; which shall be accompanied by a recommendation from at least three Lodges nearest the place in which the new Lodge is to be holden, certifying to the truth of the statements contained in said petition; and also certifying that the request for said recommendation was submitted to each Lodge at a regular meeting at least one lunar month previous to its final action thereon; together with a certificate from the Grand Lecturer, or from the Deputy Grand Master of the District that the brothers named for Master and Wardens are qualified to open and close a Lodge, and confer the three degrees of Ancient Craft Masonry.

SEC. 31. There shall be paid for every Dispensation for a new Lodge the sum of fifty dollars; for every charter the sum of one hundred dollars; from which shall be deducted the sum previously paid for Dispensation.

SEC. 32. No charter shall issue to a Lodge under Dispensation until at least four months after the date of said Dispensation, and until it shall have conferred the degrees of E. A., F. C., and M. M. in manner and form as prescribed by the rules and regulations of this Grand Lodge, and all Lodges under Dispensation shall make returns of work accompanied by their Dispensations at any annual communication of the Grand Lodge which may convene between the date of the dispensation and issuing of a charter.

SEC. 33. Lodges under Dispensation shall not elect any officers, transact any business or perform any work except that clearly expressed in the warrant of Dispensation creating them, and shall always act in strict accordance with the rules and regulations of this Grand Lodge.

SEC. 34. At least ten days before the annual communication of the Grand Lodge, all Lodges under Dispensation shall forward to the Grand Secretary their Lodge records, which shall contain a full and exact report of everything done by authority of their warrant of Dispensation, together with the Dispensation under which they have worked.

SEC. 35. Lodges under Dispensation shall be governed by such By-Laws as are enacted by this Grand Lodge.

Chartered Lodges.

SEC. 36. No Lodge chartered by this Grand Lodge shall proceed to work until the election and installation of its officers, and the constitution and dedication of the Lodge.

SEC. 37. At the first election subsequent to the issuing of a charter, any member of the Lodge possessing the qualifications required by Section 2, of Article V. of Grand Lodge Regulations, or who shall have served as Master or Warden in such Lodge, shall be eligible and may be elected to the office of Master without having previously held such office in a chartered Lodge.

SEC. 38. All Lodges in this jurisdiction shall provide suitable jewels, furniture, and clothing, and keep their Lodge rooms at all times secure and in good order.

SEC. 39. All Lodges in this jurisdiction shall, within thirty days after each annual election of officers, report to the Grand Secretary the names of the Master, Wardens, and other elected officers; the report to be signed by the Master and attested by the Secretary, under the seal of the Lodge.

SEC. 40. The books, accounts, and reports of Lodges in this jurisdiction shall cover and include the calendar year, from the first day of January to the thirty-first day of December, and it shall be the duty of the Secretary of each Lodge to make an annual report to the Grand Secretary before the tenth day of January in each year, of the names of the Master, Wardens, and officers of the Lodge, a list of those initiated, passed, raised, admitted, restored, dimitted, deaths, suspensions, expulsions, and rejections, with the respective dates opposite each name; also the number of miles necessarily traveled by its representative to attend the communication of the Grand Lodge; the returns to be signed by the Master.

SEC. 41. This Grand Lodge may require the Secretary and Treasurer of any Lodge in its jurisdiction, or any constituent Lodge may require these officers to give bonds with sufficient sureties to this Grand Lodge for the faithful performance of their respective duties and trusts, in accordance with the "Act of Incorporation" and "Corporate By-Laws" of this Grand Lodge.

SEC. 42. Any Lodge in this jurisdiction authorized to conduct its business and confer the degrees of Ancient Craft Masonry in a foreign language, may make no change or modification in the work or lectures, and is required to keep all records, and make all reports and returns to the Grand Lodge in the English language; and the Master and Wardens of any such Lodge shall be familiar with and well-skilled in the work and lectures in the English language.

SEC. 43. If any Lodge in this jurisdiction shall cease to exist, the last Master or Wardens shall within sixty days thereafter transmit to the Grand Secretary all the books, papers, jewels, furniture, funds, and other property or evidences thereof, of the Lodge so ceasing to exist.

SEC. 44. No Lodge can surrender its charter without the consent of this Grand Lodge, or of the Grand Master, so long as there are eight Master Masons, members thereof, who desire to work under said charter according to the Regulations of this Grand Lodge and the usages of Masonry.

SEC. 45. Whenever the charter of a Lodge shall in any manner be destroyed, or shall become so defaced and illegible as to be unfit for use, or shall be stolen or surreptitiously taken and detained, without the fault of the Lodge or Master, it shall be the duty of the Grand Master to suspend its powers, and it shall be lawful for the Grand Master to order another charter to be issued to said Lodge, which charter shall bear the same name and number, setting forth the names of the members and officers named in the first charter, the date thereof, the names of the Grand Officers attached thereto, and the reasons for granting another charter, which shall be signed by the Grand Master and attested by the Grand Secretary under his hand and the Seal of the Grand Lodge, without fee.

Charity.

SEC. 46. No applications made to this Grand Lodge for charity or relief shall be acted upon until they have been first referred to the Finance Committee, and their report received by the Grand Lodge.

SEC. 47. No Lodge in this jurisdiction, or officer or member thereof shall give any certificate or recommendation to enable a Mason in an itinerant manner to apply to Lodges for relief.

Masonic Emblems.

SEC. 48. The use of Masonic emblems by Masons as business signs or cards, unless such business be exclusively or largely in Masonic goods, is strictly prohibited.

Adopted by the Grand Lodge of F. & A. M., of the State of Michigan, in Grand Communication held at Detroit, on the 16th day of January A. L. 5873; and ordered to take effect on the first day of July, A. L. 5873, A. D. 1873.

RULES OF ORDER

FOR THE

GOVERNMENT OF GRAND LODGE.

Rule 1. The Roll of Officers and Members shall be called at the opening of each day's session, and no member, who shall fail to be present, shall be entitled to *per diem* allowance, unless his absence shall be excused by the Grand Master.

2. None but members of the Grand Lodge, past or present officers of other Grand Lodges excepted, shall be present at the opening of the same; nor shall any visitor be admitted during the session, except by permission of the Grand Master.

3. All members and visitors shall keep the seats assigned them, except those officers whose duties may call them about the Lodge.

4. All resolutions shall be submitted in writing before there shall be any debate upon them; as shall all motions, if the Grand Master or any brother desire it.

5. All matters in Grand Lodge are to be decided by vote, each member having one vote only, unless the question be taken by ballot or by the calling of Lodges, when, if he be entitled to three votes, he may give them. The Grand Master shall be entitled to one vote on all questions, and may also give the casting vote whenever there shall be an equal division.

6. The Grand Master shall order a call of Lodges on all questions, on which the Constitution or By-Laws of the Grand Lodge require by a vote of yeas and nays, and, on any other question, when such vote is demanded by the Representatives of fifty Lodges.

7. Each member shall vote on all questions except when he is personally interested, unless specially excused by the Grand Lodge.

8. No brother shall speak more than twice to the same question, unless in explanation, without permission of the Grand Master.

9. Every member who speaks shall rise and remain standing, addressing himself to the Grand Master; nor shall any brother presume to interrupt him, except on a point of order.

10. When a question is under debate, no motion shall be received, except to amend, commit, lay upon the table, or adjourn.

11. A motion to amend, until decided, shall preclude all other amendments of the main question.

12. Any member may call for a division of the question when the same will admit of it.

13. No new motion which totally changes the subject matter on which the original motion was intended to operate, shall be admitted under color of amendment, as a substitute for the motion under debate.

14. No member, except one of the majority which decided the question, shall be allowed to move for a reconsideration.

15. After a motion is stated by the Grand Master, it shall be deemed to be in possession of the Grand Lodge, but may be withdrawn by the mover at any time before decision or amendment.

16. There shall be no debate upon any question after it is put by the Grand Master.

17. All motions and reports may be committed at the pleasure of the Grand Lodge.

18. While the Grand Master is addressing the Grand Lodge, or putting a question, or a brother speaking, no member shall entertain any private discourse, nor pass between the speaker and the chair.

19. All communications, petitions, appeals, resolutions, propositions, and motions, shall be couched in decent and respectful language, or they shall not be entertained in Grand Lodge.

20. No Brother shall leave the Grand Lodge during the session without permission of the Grand Master.

Adopted January 16th, A. L. 5873; to take effect July 1st, A. L. 5873.

DEFINITIONS.

(*INFORMALLY APPROVED BY GRAND LODGE.*)

In Ample Form—The Grand Lodge is declared to be opened or closed in Ample Form when the Grand Master presides;

In Due Form—When the Deputy Grand Master presides; and

In Form—When it is opened or closed in the absence of both the Grand Master and his Deputy.

Dimitted Mason—Is a Master Mason in good standing, but who has no membership in a Lodge.

Reprimand—Is the lowest penalty inflicted upon Masons who have been found guilty of a Masonic offense. It must be pronounced by the Master in open Lodge.

Suspension—Excludes a Brother from all Masonic privileges, and prohibits all Masonic intercourse with him during the time of his suspension.

Expulsion—The highest penalty that can be incurred, and the severest punishment that can be inflicted for any violation of Masonic engagements. It excludes a Mason from all his Masonic rights and privileges forever, unless he be restored by the Lodge or Grand Lodge.

Notification—Is the notice by which the time, place, and hour, (and frequently the business,) of the Lodge are communicated to the members. This notice, every Brother receiving it is expected to obey, unless his doing so would materially interfere with his business engagements. It is also called *due and timely notice.*

A Summons—Is a call of authority; a citation to appear and answer to the charges therein set forth. Or it is an imperative injunction to appear at a meeting of the Lodge with which the

Brother receiving it is affiliated; or to attend on the Grand Master, the District Deputy Grand Master, or any Committee or other body authorized by the Grand Lodge to issue it. The obligation to obey it is special and obligatory on every Brother receiving it. The penalty for not obeying is expulsion, unless the party offending be able to urge a pressing and positive necessity for his excuse.

Member of a Lodge—Is a Master Mason who has been *raised*, or who, by vote, has been admitted to membership. Signing the By-Laws is not necessary to perfect membership.

Honorary Member—Of a Lodge is a Master Mason who has been elected as such, in compliment to his high personal and Masonic character. He acquires no privilege in the Lodge except the right to sit therein, and shall be exempt from the payment of assessments and dues, and the honorary relation ceases if he fail to maintain membership in a chartered Lodge.

The Lodge—This term is generally understood to refer to the members of a particular Masonic body, or the place in which they meet. The *flooring*, or Master's carpet, is frequently called the Lodge.

The Master's Carpet—Is a regularly arranged painting of the Masonic emblems employed in our ritual, which no Lodge can be without.

BLANK FORMS.

(Prepared by the Committee on the Revision of the Constitution and published herewith, by order of the Grand Lodge.)

NO. 1.

WARRANT OF A D. D. GRAND MASTER.

GRAND LODGE OF MICHIGAN, F. AND A. M.

To all Lodges and Brethren to whom these Presents may come, Greeting:

Reposing especial confidence in the Masonic Fidelity, Zeal, and Ability of W. Bro.--------------------------------------, I have appointed him D. D. Grand Master in and for the ------------ Masonic District of this Grand Jurisdiction; and he is hereby clothed with all the Powers conferred on a D. D. Grand Master by the Constitution and By-Laws of this Grand Lodge; and all Lodges and Brethren, within said Masonic District, are hereby commanded to receive and respect him accordingly: this Warrant to be and remain in full force and effect until the last day of the Annual Communication of this Grand Lodge next succeeding the date hereof, unless sooner revoked, of which, all Lodges of the District shall have due and timely notice.

{SEAL} In testimony whereof, I have hereunto subscribed my name, and caused the Seal of this Grand Lodge to be affixed, on this --------------- day of--------------A. L. 58--

----
Grand Master.

ATTEST:

Grand Secretary.

NO. 2.

CERTIFICATE OF OFFICERS ELECTED BY LODGE.

We hereby certify, that at a Regular Communication of------------Lodge, No. ----, holden at -------------, on the ------------ day of --------------, A. L. 58--, the following named Brothers were duly elected to the several offices named, and are now installed, and in the performance of their respective duties.

Bro. --, Worshipful Master.
Bro: --, Senior Warden.
Bro. --, Junior Warden.
Bro. --, Treasurer.
Bro. --, Secretary.

{SEAL} In testimony whereof, we have set our hands hereto, and caused the Seal of the Lodge to be hereto affixed, at ------------------------, this-------------- day of--------------, A. L. 58--

----
W. Master.

Secretary.

NO. 3.

NOTICE TO CONTIGUOUS LODGES.

------------ LODGE, NO. ----, OF F: AND A. MASONS, }
---------------------------- A. L. 58---. }

To the Secretary of ---------- Lodge, No. ---, F. and A. Masons:

DEAR SIR AND BROTHER,—Your Lodge is hereby notified that at a Regular Communication of ---------------------- Lodge No ----, held as above. (Mr. or Bro.)------------------------------------- was *-------------------------

By order of the Lodge.

{SEAL}

Yours Fraternally,

-------------------------------------,
Secretary.

*Insert here, as the case may require, *Rejected*, *Suspended*, *Expelled*, or *Restored*.

NO. 4.

PETITION FOR INITIATION.

To the Worshipful Master, Wardens and Brethren of ---------------Lodge No -- of Free and Accepted Masons:

The subscriber, residing at ------------------, and whose place of business is at------------------, being ---- years of age; and by occupation a------------; and having---------- applied for initiation to --------------- Lodge No.--------- respectfully represents that, unbiased by friends and uninfluenced by mercenary motives, he freely and voluntarily offers himself as a candidate for the Mysteries of Masonry; and that he is prompted to solicit this privilege by a favorable opinion of your ancient and honorable Fraternity, a desire for knowledge, and sincere wish to be serviceable to his fellow creatures; and should his petition be granted, he will cheerfully conform to all its established laws, usages and customs.

Dated ----------------, A. L. 58--

Recommended by

--------------------------------------- }
--------------------------------------- } -------------------------------------

[On the back of which shall be the following:]

Application of --------------------------- Recommended by-------------------
Petition Received---A. L. 58------
Referred to--, Com.
Elected--A. L. 58------

NO. 5.

PETITION FOR ADVANCEMENT.

To the Worshipful Master, Wardens and Brethren of ---------- Lodge No. ----, F. & A. M.:

The subscriber, a ---------------- having received the degree of ------------ in---------------- Lodge, No. ----, under the jurisdiction of the Grand Lodge of --------------, respectfully petitions for advancement in your Lodge, and if found worthy he pledges himself to a cheerful compliance with the Rules and Regulations of the Fraternity. Accompanying his petition is a certificate from ---------------- Lodge, No. ----, recommending and consentiug that his petition be granted.

His age is ---- years; occupation --------------; residence -----------------

Signed ---------------------------------------

Recommended by---------------------------------------

NO. 6.

PETITION FOR MEMBERSHIP.

To the Worshipful Master, Wardens and Brethren of ---------- Lodge No. ----, F. & A. M.:

The subscriber a Master Mason, and late a member of------------Lodge, No, ----, under the jurisdiction of the Grand Lodge of ----------, respectfully petitions for membership in your Lodge; if found worthy, he pledges himself to a cheerful obedience of your By-Laws and the ancient usages of Masonry. Accompanying his petition is---------------------------------------

His age is ---- years; occupation ------------; residence-------------------

Signed. --------------------------------

Recommended by

[In all cases where the petition for membership is rejected, the certificate of Dimit, or other documentary evidence accompanying it must be returned to the Petitioner; if the candidate be elected, such Dimit or documentary evidence must be cancelled and filed by the Secretary of the Lodge.]

NO. 7.

REPORT OF A COMMITTEE, ON A PETITION FOR INITIATION.

To the Worshipful Master, Wardens and Brethren of ----------------Lodge No -- of Free and Accepted Masons:

The Committee to whom was referred the petition of----------------for ----------------, upon diligent inquiry, report as follows:

That he is ---- physically competent for admission;

He has ---- resided within the jurisdiction of this Lodge for the last twelve months.

His belief is ---- in God;

Is occupation is----------------------------:

His company and associates are ---- of a respectable character;

He is ---- addicted to the intemperate use of intoxicating liquors;

He uses ---- profane language:

He has ---- licentious nor immoral habits.

All of which is respectfully submitted.

---------------------------- } *Committee.*

------------------------------A. L. 58--.

[On the back of which shall be the following:]

Petition of------------------------------, For-----------------------------------
Presented --18----
Committee --
Report ---
Please return this to the Secretary's desk, on or before------------------18----

NO. 8.

FORM OF CERTIFICATE OF DIMIT.

------------------------------------ LODGE, NUMBER ---- OF F. & A. M.

To all Free and Accepted Masons, Greeting:

The Master and Wardens of-------------------Lodge, No. ----, F. & A. M., working under a Charter from the M. W. G. Lodge of the State of Michigan, do hereby certify that Bro. ----------------, (who has written his name on the Margin of this Certificate,) is a Master Mason, in good and regular standing; and is hereby, at his own request, Discharged from Membership in our said Lodge.

{SEAL} In testimony whereof, we have hereunto subscribed our names, and caused the Seal of our said Lodge to be affixed at---------- in the County of-----------------------, and State of Michigan, this---------- day of ------------ A. D. 18----, A. L. 58----

--------------------------W. M.

ATTEST:

-----------------------------, Secretary.

NO. 9.

FORM OF PROXY TO GRAND LODGE.

This is to certify that at a regular communication of ---------------------- Lodge, No. ----, F. & A. M., held at------------, Michigan,------------ A. L. 58----, Bro. -------------------, a member of this Lodge, was elected to represent said Lodge at the next succeeding session of the M. W. Grand Lodge of the State of Michigan.

[SEAL.] Signed. ---------------------------, W. M.

Attest: ------------------------------, Secy.

Dated, ------------------------------, 58--

STANDING ORDERS AND RESOLUTIONS

OF THE

GRAND LODGE, F. and A. M.

OF THE

STATE OF MICHIGAN.

---

1. *Resolved*, That no officer presiding in any Lodge within the jurisdiction of this Grand Lodge is entitled to wear any regalia, except that of a Master Mason; and any attempt to introduce any other is an innovation upon the long established usages of Masonry, and one that cannot receive the sanction of this Grand Lodge, and is hereafter expressly prohibited.

2. *Resolved*, That the following Masonic clothing and insignia be established as the standard in this jurisdiction; and that all Lodges and Brethren, hereafter procuring new clothing, be recommended to have the same made in conformity with the following description, to wit:

JEWELS.—The Jewels of officers of Lodges, shall be the same as are now in use, of a pattern to be found in the Grand Secretary's office.

COLLARS.—Of officers of Lodges, to be of light blue ribbon or velvet, four inches broad.

APRONS.—*Entered Apprentice.*—A plain white lamb skin or linen, from fourteen to sixteen inches wide, twelve to fourteen inches deep, square at bottom, and without ornament; white strings, with a flap or fall, to be triangular in shape.

Fellow-Craft.—The same, with the addition only of two sky-blue rosettes at the bottom.

Master-Mason.—The same, with sky-blue lining and edging, one-and-a-half inches deep, and an additional rosette on the fall or flap, and silver tassels. No other color or ornament shall be allowed, except to officers of Lodges who may have the emblems of their office, in silver or white, in the centre of the apron.

The Masters and Past Masters of Lodges to wear, in lieu and in the place of the three rosettes on the Master Mason's apron, perpendicular lines upon horizontal lines, thereby forming three several sets of two right angles, the length of the horizontal lines to be two inches and a half each, and of the perpendicular lines, one inch; these emblems to be of ribbon or silver, half an inch broad, and if ribbon, of the same color of the lining and edging of the apron.

3. *Resolved*, That the Grand Treasurer be, and he is hereby authorized and fully empowered, in the name of the Grand Lodge of Free and Accepted Masons of the State of Michigan, to collect, by legal proceedings or otherwise, any debt due the Grand Lodge, whenever, in his opinion, the interests of the Grand Lodge shall require such action.

4. *Resolved*, That the Master or Wardens of a Lodge, in case of permanent removal from the Jurisdiction, are entitled to dimit, under like restrictions as other members of their Lodge.

5. *Resolved*, That all members [Masons?] in the jurisdiction of this Grand Lodge be and are hereby interdicted and prohibited from forming incorporate bodies [Lodges?] under the laws of this State.

6. *Resolved*, That the R. W. Grand Lecturer be authorized to recommend, and the M. W. Grand Master to appoint under the seal of this Grand Lodge, such assistant lecturers as may be necessary, whose jurisdiction shall be set forth in said appointment, whose duty it shall be to visit all Lodges in their jurisdiction at least once in each year, or oftener, if in his opinion, it is necessary, and instruct the several Lodges in the work and lectures; said assistants shall be paid by the Lodges for such services: Provided that they shall not demand to exceed five dollars for any one visit, and that all Lodges within this Grand Jurisdiction are strictly enjoined to conform to the work and lectures, as taught by said Grand Lecturer and his assistants duly appointed.

7. *Resolved*, That all Lodges within this Jurisdiction are enjoined and prohibited from encouraging, promoting or permitting the delivery or teaching of any Masonic lectures or work which are not sanctioned or authorized by this Grand Lodge in accordance with its Constitution; and all Brothers within this Jurisdiction are prohibited from delivering or teaching such lectures to Lodges in this State.

8. *Resolved*, That when it shall come to the knowledge of of the M. W. Grand Master that a subordinate Lodge is suffering

from confusion, discord, or other mismanagement, through the inefficiency or improper conduct of its W. M., or other officers, that the M. W. Grand Master shall have power, and it shall be his duty, to appoint a proxy to take charge of such Lodge, and to conduct the same as such proxy representing the M. W. Grand Master, until the next Grand Communication thereafter.

9. *Resolved*, That each Lodge receiving a Dispensation, is required to record the same in its books of record, before proceeding to do any work or transact any business by virtue of the powers thereby conferred.

10. *Resolved*, That all newly chartered Lodges may hold their first election of officers at any Regular Communication within two months after the date of their Charter.

11. *Resolved*, That neither three of the Masonic penalties should be inflicted upon a Brother without charges, specifications, notice and trial in due Masonic form.

12. *Resolved*, That in Masonry the accuser of a Brother Mason must be a Master Mason in good standing, who need not be sworn. The complaint or testimony of persons not Masons may be taken before the examining committee, on oath or otherwise, as the Lodge shall direct; but the testimony of witnesses not Masons should be taken before a committee, and not in open Lodge.

13. *Resolved*, That no appeal from a Subordinate Lodge shall be entertained by the Grand Lodge, except upon proof that notice of said appeal has been given to the Subordinate Lodge in writing, within ninety days after the appellant shall have received official notice of such decision; and such appeal shall be prosecuted at the first Regular Communication of the Grand Lodge after the time above limited shall have expired.

14. *Resolved*, That accusations or charges against members of a Lodge, or against Subordinate Lodges, can not be received from nonaffiliated Masons, except in case of charges against a member of a Lodge by leave granted by a vote of such Lodge, and in case of charges against a Subordinate Lodge, by leave of the Grand Lodge.

15. Charges having been preferred, and the Committee having reported, can the accused be expelled at any but a Regular Communication?

[Action on the charges must be commenced at a Regular Communication, and may be continued from time to time, and had at Special Communications, convened for that purpose, by vote at such Regular, or notice to all the members of the Lodge within the jurisdiction.]

16. *Resolved*, That it is the right of a Subordinate Lodge to require of a member suspended for non-payment of dues, as a condition of restoration, the payment of a sum equal to the amount of dues during the term of suspension, in addition to his dues at the time of his suspension.

17. *Resolved*, That no Lodge shall receive any petition for initiation, unless the applicant state in the petition whether he has ever applied for initiation to any other Lodge, and if such application has been made, shall state the time or times when, and the Lodge or Lodges to which such application has been made; and in case such statements are found to be false, it shall be good cause for expulsion from the Order.

18. *Resolved*, That it shall be the duty of W. M. of every Subordinate Lodge to cause the Constitution and Standing Orders of this Grand Lodge to be read at their respective Lodges, at least once in three months.

DECISIONS

OF

GRAND MASTER M'CURDY.

(MADE SINCE THE ADOPTION OF THE CONSTITUTION, REGULATIONS, ETC.,) AND APPROVED BY GRAND LODGE.

Question. Can a subordidate Lodge collect dues from non-affiliated Masons residing within its jurisdiction?

In reply to the foregoing question I would state, the first action of the Grand Lodge upon this subject was passed in 1856 (see Proc. of 1856, page 55) which, after authorizing "disciplinary control," etc., provides that the Lodges have the right to demand and receive dues from such non-affiliated Masons and to suspend them for the non-payment of the same." The next action was taken in 1869, (see Proc. of 1869, page 54) when the Lodges were authorized and required "to collect such dues," and the mode of discipline provided upon refusal. This legislation has never been enforced, but has always been regarded and treated as void. For my own part, I always considered the action of the Grand Lodge upon this subject in direct contravention of the ancient landmarks of the craft.

The whole subject of dues is constitutionally within the exclusive jurisdiction of the Lodge, and relates *solely to its members*, as a consideration for the enjoyment of privileges which appertain to membership only. If these resolutions could be enforced, they would compel payment of dues by even those who are debarred from visiting the Lodge more than three times.

It would be demanding payment for a consideration which, while the Lodge enforced it upon the one hand, it might at the same time deny the right of visitation on the other.

Non-affiliants have *obligations to perform as well as rights that must be respected.*

Look's Masonic Digest. page 69.

Chase's Digest Masonic Law, page 173.

Lockwood's Digest Masonic Law, page 36.

Mackey's Digest Masonic Jurisprudence, pages 194 and 275.

I have thus fully stated the action of our Grand Lodge upon the subject, that the craft may know what has been done; also that my answer, to the question propounded, may not seem to override the action of the Grand Lodge; because, admitting the resolutions to be valid, I am of the opinion that they were repealed upon the adoption of the Constitution of 1866. Section 13, article 5, provides what jurisdiction the Lodges shall have over non-affiliated Masons residing within their respective jurisdiction, and hence by fair construction excludes any other than that which is specified. Section 6, article 6, confers upon every Lodge full power to regulate its own internal police, by the adoption of a Constitution, By-Laws and other regulations not inconsistent with the provisions of the Constitution or the ancient usages of the fraternity.

The Constitution adopted at the last session of the Grand Lodge and which becomes operative July 1st, 1873, confers upon constituent Lodges substantially the rights and powers of the present one. Section 7, of article 2, declares the right of a Lodge to "make its own By-Laws, fixing the annual dues of its members"—not to fix annual dues on non-affiliants; and section 5, of article 19, gives non-affiliates the privilege to visit a Lodge not more than three times. This legislation is consistent; the Constitution of 1866, and the last one adopted, are in perfect accord and in harmony with the rights and pererogatives of Lodges, as well as those which appertain to non-affiliates. I am, therefore, of the opinion that a Lodge, Grand or Subordinate, has no Masonic right to collect dues from non-affiliate Masons residing within its jurisdiction.

Question. Is it proper to pass the ballot to advance a candidate at any other than a Regular Communication, he having been rejected at a Special Communication?

Answer. After the application of a candidate for advancement has been rejected by a Lodge having jurisdiction, he can renew such application only at some succeeding regular meeting thereof. Sec. 1, Art. 17, Regulations.

Question. Is it proper for a Lodge to confer the degrees upon a candidate who can neither read nor write?

Answer. A candidate who cannot *read* or cannot *write* is not a fit and proper subject to be make a Mason; further, the second subdivision of section 1, article 14, of the Regulations, requires the petitioner (for initiation) to *to sign his name in full to the petition.* This can be done by no other person than himself; it cannot be done by an attorney. I therefore hold that a candidate who cannot *both read and write is not qualified to be a Mason.*

[The following decisions relate to questions arising since the new G. L. Constitution, Regulations, and By-Laws took effect, July 1st, 1873:]

Question. Does Masonry require a candidate to avow a belief in the Divine authenticity of the Holy Scriptures?

Answer. No. Symbolic Masonry acknowledges God, and demands of its votaries a declaration of belief in the *existence* of God—Jehovah—a Supreme Being. This is demanded because we seek Masonic association only with those whose moral natures and conduct are restrained, and whose Masonic obligations are made binding by such belief.

But Masonry is not a religion, nor is it a sect, neither does it enforce any theological *interpretation* upon a Mason's belief. Its demands in this respect are fully satisfied when the existence of God is acknowledged as *a fact.* It, in like spirit, accepts the earth, the sun, the moon, the stars, and man himself as *facts*, and does not require any interpretation of the facts. The Indian who believes in the "Great Spirit," and the Jew who reverently adores the "Great Jehovah"—the Trinitarian and Unitarian—the Calvinist and Armenian—the Catholic and the Protestant—the Mahommedan and the Hindoo, can all harmoniously kneel at Masonic altars and recognize their mutual fraternal relations. This is so, because each knows that every other brother, who kneels there has avowed his belief in the existence of a Supreme Being, and, furthermore, because each one knows that his own *interpretation* of his own belief will not be questioned or challenged, neither will his freedom of conscience be restricted or controlled by Masons or Masonry.

This is one of the grand secrets of that wonderful vitality which Masonry has always shown, from its origin in a remote antiquity down through all the variations and divisions of religious belief, until the present day; when we see within its mystic fold, the representatives of nearly every race and nation, and the disciples of nearly every faith in the known world. And it is because Masonry permits us thus to meet at her altars as *men* —as the representatives of a common humanity—and as brothers who trace their origin to a Universal Father, that it is the only human institution which presents the sublime spectacle of a really universal brotherhood.

While our landmarks admit no Atheist to our ranks, they do not authorize us to demand of a candidate or a brother any declaration of his specific belief concerning the origin of the Holy Scriptures, the manner of their communication to man, or the precise signification of their contents. We, as Masons, do not undertake to decide questions on which theologians themselves do not agree. The Bible, the Square and the Compasses are recognized lights in Masonry; and we have no more right to demand that the Mason or the candidate shall declare what he believes to be the origin or the nature of the Bible than we have to require him to declare what he believes to be the origin or the nature of the metal in the square. The former we leave to the theologian and to every man's conscience, and the latter to the chemist and to every man's investigation. The uses we make of these Masonic lights *do not require* that these questions be mooted or decided by us.

Inasmuch, therefore, as our landmarks do not demand of the candidate any declaration of *faith or of religious belief*, except that of the existence of God—a Supreme Being—the Great Ruler of the Universe;

It is ordered that the Lodges of this Grand Jurisdiction can neither *add to nor take from* the requirements, in this respect, which were established by our ancient brethren.

Question. What power has a Lodge over material rejected by it prior to and since the time the new Regulations took effect?

Answer. A Lodge has personal jurisdiction over its rejected material, whether rejected prior or subsequent to the adoption of the new Regulations, and "has the exclusive right to accept it wherever residing; but it may waive this right." [See Art. XII., sub-section 4.]

Section 3, of article XIII. of the Regulations provides that "no Lodge shall initiate an applicant who has been rejected by another Lodge, in this or any other Grand Jurisdiction until the rejecting Lodge shall have given its unanimous recommendation and consent thereto by a secret ballot at a regular meeting.

And section 1, of article XVII., states that "a candidate who has been rejected by a Lodge having jurisdiction may renew his application to the same Lodge at any succeeding regular meeting thereof; but if such applicant change his residence he shall apply to a Lodge of the jurisdiction in which he resides; but such Lodge shall not confer any degree on such applicant without the recommendation and consent thereto of the Lodge having personal jurisdiction of the material."

These three sections appear to conflict with each other.

1. Subdivision four, supra, gives a Lodge "the *exclusive right* to accept its rejected material."

2. Section 3, article 13, prohibits a Lodge initiating an applicant who has been rejected by another Lodge, "until the rejecting Lodge shall have given its unanimous consent thereto by a secret ballot at a regular meeting."

3. Section 1, of article XVII. says "if such applicant change his residence (*i. e.* if such candidate, after rejection, change his residence) he shall apply to a Lodge of the jurisdiction in which he resides; but such Lodge shall not confer any degree on such applicant without the recommendation and consent thereto of the Lodge having personal jurisdiction of the material." In construing a law, such construction should always be given to it as will render all its provisions operative and consistent, if possible; and, if different portions seem to conflict, to render them harmonious. From the foregoing proposition it is evident, *first*, that no Lodge can *accept* the rejected material of another Lodge until that Lodge has waived its personal jurisdiction; *second*, that no Lodge can initiate an applicant (it may receive his petition) who has been rejected by another Lodge until its unanimous consent is given; *third*, that the rejected candidate may apply to the Lodge rejecting him at any succeeding regular meeting thereof, although such candidate may have changed his resi-

dence and reside within the jurisdiction of another Lodge; or he may apply to the Lodge in whose jurisdiction he resides. The language of section 1, article XVII. is, "if a candidate change his residence after he has been rejected, he shall apply to a Lodge of the jurisdiction in which he resides." Here the word "*shall*" has only the force and effect of the word *may*, and gives the candidate a choice: to apply to the Lodge originally rejecting him, or to any Lodge under whose jurisdiction he may happen to reside. The Lodge receiving the petition of a candidate under such circumstances may act upon it, and elect or reject; if it should elect, it shall not confer any degree on such applicant without the recommendation and the consent thereto of the Lodge having personal jurisdiction of the material.

I decide, therefore, that Lodges have personal jurisdiction of their rejected material—rejected prior as well as subsequent to the first day of July last; also, that when a candidate, who may have been rejected by one Lodge, removes into the jurisdiction of another, such other Lodge can receive and act upon his application; but if the applicant be elected, such Lodge shall take no further action until it shall have obtained the recommendation and consent of the Lodge having personal jurisdiction of the rejected material.

Question. Can a Lodge remit the dues of one or more of its own members for life?

Answer. No. Such action would tend to embarrass the Lodge, retard its successful operation and create confusion among the craft. Every Lodge must necessarily incur expense in maintaining an existence and in executing its functions; and justice and right demand that such expense should be paid equally by every brother (unless exempt under *certain circumstances*) who exercises and enjoys the benefits and privileges of the Lodge. A Lodge has the power "*to fix the annual dues of its members*," not to exempt them from the payment of dues; but it may *remit* the dues of a member on "charitable considerations." There is an important distinction to ke kept in view in these two classes; first, no dues *accrue* against a brother *exempt* from the payment of dues; in order to remit dues the obligation to pay a certain sum must actually exist before the Lodge can remit the same.

If every Lodge should remit or exempt its members from the payment of dues for life, what would become of a Lodge and

Grand Lodge revenues? The answer is apparent. It is ordered that a Lodge cannot remit the dues of its own members for life, but it may, from time to time, remit dues on charitable considerations.

See Article 2, clause 2, sub-section 7, of Grand Lodge Regulations. By-Laws Grand Lodge, section 26, fifth subdivision.

Question. Can a Lodge make honorary members of its own members, without their retaining full membership in their own Lodge, and paying dues?

Answer. This question involves two propositions. The last proposition relating to dues being fully disposed of by the answer to the preceding question, the question that remains to be considered is this, "Can a Lodge make honorary members of its own members?" It cannot. Honorary membership is incident to actual membership and is dependent upon it; therefore, when a brother is an actual member of a Lodge he is in the enjoyment of all the privileges and of the *highest privileges it can bestow*.

Honorary membership may be conferred by a Lodge upon those who are *members of other Lodges*, but not upon its own members.

Question. A petition for initiation is received and referred to a committee; at the next regular meeting of the Lodge, and before the committee has reported, a motion is made to *withdraw* the petition. Is such a motion proper; if not what is the proper proceedure?

Answer. The motion to withdraw a petition is proper whenever it is in order. The usual course of procedure is this: A brother moves to discharge the committee from the further consideration of the petition, and to instruct it to return the same to the Lodge *without report*. The mover should state that his motion is preliminary to another to withdraw the petition. With this explanation all brothers vote understandingly. A majority of the brethren present may instruct the committee to return the paper to the Lodge, and when it is returned the motion to withdraw is in order, but the motion to withdraw cannot prevail unless sustained by the *unanimous vote* of the brethren present. (See 7th clause of sec. 1, art. XIV. of Regulations.)

Question. A candidate is elected to take the first degree, but before he receives it a brother of the Lodge *objects* to the degree being conferred; the petition with its accompanying fee is returned to the candidate. A few days after its return the objecting brother withdraws his objection; can I now proceed to confer the degrees without further ceremony?

Answer. No. The grand object of the law is to protect the craft. The safe and prudent course in such a case, is to inform the candidate that he can—*if he chooses*—petition the Lodge again for the honors of Masonry. A second petition gives the usual notice to the brethren, and enables them to know also that the objection has been withdrawn; after which, if they see fit, they can elect him. Too much care cannot be exercised by the craft in accepting material.

Question. A brother from another Grand Jurisdiction has petitioned my Lodge for membership, and files with his petition a dimit from his Lodge *only;* is that sufficient evidence?

Answer. No. A constituent Lodge of this Grand Jurisdiction cannot be presumed to know, except on proper evidence, that a Lodge in another Grand Jurisdiction is working under a regular and unforfeited charter. A certificate of dimit, purporting to emanate from such foreign Lodge, is not of itself sufficient evidence of the regularity and good standing of the Lodge issuing it. But if such certificate of dimit have attached thereto the certificate of the Grand Secretary under the seal of said foreign Grand Jurisdiction, that the said dimitting Lodge is regular and in good standing, the evidence required by our regulations is complete.

Question. At our last regular a brother applied verbally for his dimit aud stated his reasons for so doing; is such application sufficient?

Answer. No. It cannot be presumed that the Secretary records all that brothers may say in the Lodge. The regulations require that a brother, asking for a dimit, shall give his reasons therefor; which, if given verbally, will often fail to become a matter of record. If it be necessary to give reasons for such an important act, it is *doubly necessary* that those reasons be put in writing and subscribed by the brother himself and filed in the archives of the Lodge, as the basis of his application and a warrant for the action of the Lodge.

Question. My Lodge granted a brother a dimit; but, as the Secretary had no dimit blanks on hand, he failed to make it out and hand it to the brother; at the next regular the brother attended, and stated he had concluded not to go away and wished to remain a member of the Lodge. A motion was then made to rescind the vote granting the dimit, which I refused to entertain. Have I done right?

Answer. Yes. When the vote granting the dimit was declared, the membership was severed. If the brother desires to re-join your Lodge the dimit certificate should be made out and deposited with his petition for that purpose. The motion to rescind the former action was not in order. "The vote of the Lodge" in such case "is the dimit," and the certificate of dimit made by the Secretary is evidence only that the dimit was granted—evidence which may be furnished by the Secretary to the brother at any time after the vote by which he has been dimited, (See sections 10 and 11 of article XVI. of the Regulations.)

Question. Charges have been preferred in my Lodge against a brother who does not reside within the jurisdiction, and his residence is not known; how shall I proceed?

Answer. Order the Secretary to send a copy of the charges and summons by mail to the last known postoffice address of the accused, at least sixty days before the return day, in an envelope properly addressed, with his order endorsed thereon to return the same to him "if not delivered within ten days." If the letter be not returned to the Secretary by the Post Master it is safe to assume that it reached the person to whom it was addressed; and such service shall be taken and deemed to be sufficient.

Question. In a Masonic trial is it competent to receive evidence to impeach the general reputation of a brother in good standing?

Answer. No. The general reputation of a brother in *good standing* cannot be impeached, and every brother must be deemed and considered to be in good standing until convicted of a *Masonic offense.*

Question. At our last regular, previous to taking a vote, a number of the brothers requested that it be taken by calling the yeas and nays. I have deferred taking the vote until I know that such a vote is proper.

Answer. A vote cannot be taken in a Masonic Lodge by calling the ayes and noes. The ancient methods of voting are sufficient for all purposes, and innovations should not be permitted.

Question. Can a brother be tried for an offense committed before he was a Mason ?

Answer. It is generally conceded that he cannot; but I hold that every brother may be dealt with Masonically, for an offense involving moral turpitude committed by him previous to being made a Mason; provided, the Lodge accepting the candidate had no notice at the time of such acceptance that he was guilty of the offense charged; and, provided further, that charges be preferred against the brother within one year from the time the Lodge received such notice.

Question. Is it proper to prefer charges against a brother who is suspended?

Answer. Yes. A brother under suspension for an offense may be proceeded against for the commission of any other offense or unmasonic conduct. A sentence of suspension is not a bar to trial on an offense for which he has not been already tried and suspended.

PENAL CODE.

(See Grand Lodge Transactions for 1874, page 67.)

OFFENSES.

1. Every violation, by a Mason, of his Masonic obligations, or of the established laws, usages and customs of Masonry; every violation of the municipal law involving moral turpitude, is a Masonic offense, for which the offender may be subjected to such lawful punishment as the tribunal having jurisdiction in the case shall adjudge.

2. Masonry will not take judicial cognizance of offenses merely ecclesiastical or political in their nature, nor of a breach of contract or claim at law between Masons, or between one Mason and another, unless involving *moral* turpitude in the offender.

TRIBUNAL.

3. No Lodge shall hear or determine a Masonic trial until it shall have been regularly chartered and its officers duly elected and installed; Provided, that when any offense shall be committed within the territory of a Lodge U. D., by one not a member of a contiguous Lodge, the matter shall be referred by the Master to the Grand Master who shall have power to direct in what Lodge the offender shall be tried.

4. For the purpose of a Masonic trial, the tribunal shall consist solely of Master Masons in good standing, who are members of the Lodge in which the trial is pending.

5. The Master, or his lawful representative, shall preside at the trial. He shall decide all points of order; and all questions relating to the legality, sufficiency or regularity of any charges, or of any service, paper, or proceedings in the case; allow or forbid amendments and continuances; and control debate. No appeal

shall be taken from his decision to the Lodge, but he shall be responsible to the Grand Lodge for any abuse of his powers or error in the exercise thereof.

JURISDICTION.

6. The penal jurisdiction of a Lodge is that power which it constitutionally possesses to take judicial cognizance of Masonic offenses, and to prosecute and punish Masons therefor. A Lodge has penal jurisdiction over all Masons, affiliated and non-affiliated, residing or sojourning within its territory, and over all of its members, and over its Entered Apprentices and Fellow Crafts, wheresoever dispersed; Provided, that the Grand Master and the Master shall be exempt from the penal jurisdiction of any constituent Lodge during their term of office; but for all unmasonic or immoral acts done by either while in office, and not official in their nature, he shall be subject to the penal jurisdiction of the Lodge, when that term expires.

7. A Lodge has exclusive original jurisdiction in all cases of violation of its own By-Laws or internal regulations.

8. Conviction and punishment by a court of law shall not bar a Masonic prosecution for the same offense.

CHARGES.

9. Charges shall be made in writing (so far as proper to be written) signed by the accuser, and filed with the Secretary of the Lodge. The offense must be charged with certainty; and time place, and particulars distinctly specified. A general charge of unmasonic conduct, without specifications, shall not be received.

10. If the charges be filed at a regular communication, they shall thereupon be read by the Secretary in open Lodge; if they be filed at any other time, they shall be so read at the next regular communication after such filing. The charges shall not be amended after such reading except by permission of the Master in open Lodge.

11. Charges may be preferred only by an affiliated Master Mason in good standing. The Master, whenever he shall deem proper, may direct the Junior Warden to prefer charges.

12. When charges are preferred against an officer of the Lodge,

the Grand Master may, in his discretion, suspend the accused from office during the pendency of the trial.

13. Charges may be preferred against a Mason who is under sentence of suspension, and the Lodge may, without reinstating the accused, proceed to try and punish him for any Masonic offense other than that for which he was suspended.

14. Charges for violation of any enactment of the Grand Lodge, or of the Code, shall specify with particularity the provisions violated, as well as the facts of the violation. Where the offense is non-payment of dues, charges must be preferred and trial had as for any other Masonic offense.

15. If the charges be received, a true copy thereof shall be served upon the accused, together with a summons requiring him to appear and answer; which summons shall be made returnable at such subsequent regular communication as the Master shall direct.

16. The copy and summons may be served by any member of the Lodge. The service must be personal and at least ten days before the return day, if the place of residence of the accused is within the jurisdiction of the Lodge, and known to the Secretary; but if his residence is not known, or is beyond the jurisdiction, then the copy and summons shall be sent by mail to the last known postoffice address of the accused, at least sixty days before the return day, in an envelope properly addressed, upon which shall be endorsed an order to the Postmaster to return the same to the secretary if not delivered within ten days; and if the letter, so addressed and endorsed, be not returned by the Postmaster to the secretary, such service shall be taken and deemed to be sufficient. By the term "place of residence" shall be understood the domicil or place occupied by the accused as a home. The person making such service shall file a certificate of the time, place, and manner of making the same.

17. The accused shall be entitled to a speedy and impartial trial; and for unreasonable neglect of prosecution the Master may, in his discretion dismiss the charges.

18. The Masonic standing of the accused is not affected until after sentence. He is presumed to be innocent until proved to be guilty; and he may, at all times before sentence, vote upon all matters not involved in the charges and specifications pending

against him; Provided that he shall be debarred from visiting any but his own Lodge until after the determination of the case.

ANSWER.

19. The answer shall be in writing, unless the accused answer generally *guilty* or *not guilty*, in which case he may answer orally, and such answer shall be forthwith recorded by the Secretary. If he answer in writing, his answer shall be filed with the charges and annexed thereto.

20. If the accused neglect or refuse to answer, or stand mute, an answer of *not guilty* shall be recorded, and the trial shall proceed in all things as though he had thus answered.

COUNSEL.

21. Either the accuser or the accused may choose counsel for his assistance. None but a Master Mason in good standing shall appear as counsel.

22. The Master may appoint counsel in such case as he shall deem proper, if none be chosen. If the accused do not appear the Master shall appoint counsel for the defense, whose duty it shall be to see that the trial is fairly conducted, and the accused not unjustly imperilled.

23. A Mason under suspension can only appear in the Lodge by counsel, but he may appear personally at all meetings of Commissioners in his case.

PROOFS.

24. Upon the coming in of the answer, the Master shall appoint three Commissioners, members of the Lodge in good standing, before whom, or a majority of them, all the proofs in the case shall be taken.

25. The accused may object to any or all of the Commissioners, upon the sufficiency of which objection the Master shall decide, and make such further appointment as shall be requisite.

26. The Master has the right, by virtue of his office, to be present and preside at all meetings of the Commissioners. When present, he shall decide all questions of order and procedure; in his absence the commissioners shall decide.

27. The Commissioners shall give the accuser and accused, or their counsel, at least five days' notice of the time and place of their meeting for the taking of proofs. If the accused shall not have appeared, nor answered, he need not be notified.

28. If there be material testimony which cannot be produced before the Commissioners, the same may be taken at such other reasonable time and place, and before such other competent person or persons, as the Master shall order, five days' notice of which shall be given, as herein provided.

29. The testimony of the prosecution shall first be taken, after which the accused may introduce proofs for his defense. If any new questions be raised by the testimony for the defense, the prosecution may rebut the same, but cannot enter into any new matters unless the accused be allowed to reply to the same by counter proofs.

30. The best evidence which the circumstances admit shall be produced. All testimony that is relevant to the issue should be admitted; that which is irrelevant should be excluded. As a general rule, heresay evidence should be excluded; but in this regard an equitable discretion may be exercised.

31, Both parties shall have the right of cross-examination and objection.

32. Any discreet person is a competent witness. A witness cannot be compelled to criminate himself.

33. The official books and records of the Lodge are evidence in themselves; so also are the charter of the Lodge, and the Laws and enactments of the Lodge and the Grand Lodge.

34. The testimony of a Mason in good standing shall be taken upon his Masonic honor and obligation. The testimony of profanes shall be taken under oath, the oath to be administered by any officer competent under the law to administer oaths. The testimony of one under sentence of suspension or expulsion shall be taken in the same manner as that of a profane.

35. The attendance of witnesses who are Masons may be enforced by summons, to be issued by the Master (or his lawful representative) upon application of either party. Wilful disobedience of such summons is a Masonic offense, and shall subject the offender to discipline.

36. All of the testimony proper to be written shall be reduced to writing.

37. The Commissioners shall keep full minutes of all their proceedings, (including all motions, objections and rulings) and report them, with all the testimony, to the Lodge; but they shall report no opinion.

38. The Secretary of the Lodge (or some brother deputed in his stead by the Master) shall act as Secretary to the Commissioners. He shall fully and carefully record all proceedings pertaining to the trial that are had in the Lodge. He shall attach together all papers filed in the case, together with a report of the Commissioners in their order, with the date of filing endorsed upon each, and carefully preserve the same in the archives of the Lodge; but the same shall not be entered on record.

39. The accused shall be competent to testify in the case.

ARGUMENT.

40. Upon the reception of the report of the Commissioners, the accuser and accused have the right either in person or by counsel to argue the case before the Lodge.

41. The Master has the power to limit the parties in their argument to such time as he may deem proper, but he shall announce such limitation before the opening of the argument.

DELIBERATION.

42. Upon the conclusion of the argument (or, if there be no argument, then upon the conclusion of the testimony) the accuser (except he be the Junior Warden prosecuting officially, and in such case the party or parties directly aggrieved) and the accused, with their counsel, and every other person not authorized to vote upon the final decision of the case, shall retire from the Lodge, and the doors shall be closed for deliberation.

43. It is proper, at this stage of the proceedings, for any brother to express his views of the case, and of the law and facts involved.

JUDGEMENT.

44. Final judgment upon the guilt or innocence of the accused can only be passed in a Master Mason's Lodge. None shall be

present but those legally qualified to vote upon the case. An honorary member of the Lodge, who is not also an actual member, cannot vote nor be present.

45. The vote of the Lodge shall be first taken upon the question, "Is the accused guilty or not guilty?"

46. The vote shall be by ball ballot, and shall be taken upon each specification separately. Black shall be cast for *guilty*, and white for *not guilty*.

47. Before the ballot is taken, the Master shall see that ballots of each color, equal at least in number to the number of members present, are provided and placed in the ballot box.

48. The Master and Wardens shall inspect the ballot at the Master's station, and the result shall be declared forthwith by the Master.

49. Two-thirds of all the votes cast shall be required to convict.

50. Every brother present shall vote unless excused by the unanimous consent of the Lodge.

51. The result of the ballot upon each specification shall be recorded by the Secretary in regular order, with the numbers severally cast for *guilty* and *not guilty*. The Lodge may convict or acquit of a part or all of the specifications as they shall deem just.

52. If the accused be acquitted, the judgment of the Lodge shall be so recorded and declared forthwith. Upon a judgment of acquittal, the proceedings are absolutely terminated, and the case is closed so far as regards any further action by the Lodge. There can be no re-consideration of the vote nor re-passing of the ballot. The only remedy is by appeal to the Grand Lodge.

PENALTY.

53. After the conviction the vote shall immediately be taken upon the penalty in the following order, beginning with the highest and descending until the requisite vote is given to declare the sentence, viz:

1. Expulsion.
2. Indefinite suspension.
3. Definite suspension.
4. Reprimand.

54. If a specific penalty be provided by law for any offense, no other penalty than the one provided shall be inflicted or voted upon in such case.

55. The vote shall be by ball ballot, and shall be regulated by similar rules as in passing judgment.

56. A two-thirds vote shall be required for sentence of expulsion or suspension. Sentence of reprimand may be passed by a majority vote.

57. There shall be no re-consideration nor repassing of any ballot taken in the course of a Masonic trial.

58. Only one of the Masonic penalties shall be inflicted in any case, nor shall any other punishment be inflicted than is herein provided. A Mason shall not be expelled for non-payment of dues.

59. The result of the ballot upon each penalty shall be entered at large upon the record, with the number of votes for and against in each instance, and in the order in which the proceedings occur.

60. At the conclusion of the ballot upon the penalty, the accuser and counsel shall be re-admitted to the Lodge, and the Master shall announce the result.

61. The parties shall at once be notified of the action of the Lodge. All cases of expulsion and suspension shall be reported by the Secretary to the Grand Secretary of the Grand Lodge and to contiguous Lodges. If the person expelled or suspended were a member of another Lodge than the one in which he was tried, the Lodge of which he was a member shall be immediately notified of the sentence, and the cause of the same, by the Secretary.

APPEALS

62. Any brother deeming himself aggrieved by the decision of the Lodge, of the Master thereof, or of the Commissioners, may appeal to the Grand Lodge. All appeals shall be in writing, and shall set forth clearly the ground upon which the appellant seeks redress.

63. The appeal may be taken whether the accused be convicted or acquitted, and by either party. It applies as well in questions of law as in questions of fact, and may be taken from any erro-

neous action, ruling or decision of the Lodge, the Master or the Commissioners.

64. The appeal must be taken, and notice thereof given in writing to the Lodge, by filing the same with the Secretary, within forty days after the appellant shall have notice of the decision from which the appeal is taken.

65. Upon receipt of the notice of appeal the Secretary shall immediately make and transmit to the Grand Secretary full and accurate copies duly certified, of all the proceedings in the case as they are recorded upon the books of the Lodge, and of the charges and specifications, answer or answers, notices, summonses, proofs, reports, and all papers of every kind in the archives of the Lodge pertaining to the subject matter. He shall minute upon the record the receipt of the notice of appeal, and the date of his return to the Grand Lodge.

66. The appeal shall be prosecuted at the first Annual Communication of the Grand Lodge, after the time limited for taking the same shall have expired. Any appeal not prosecuted as aforesaid shall, on motion, be dismissed by the Grand Lodge, unless good cause for the delay appear. After such dismissal the Masonic standing of the accused shall be the same as though no appeal had been taken.

67. If, after appeal is taken, either party desires to introduce new evidence, he shall apply to the Grand Master, stating the nature of the same. The Grand Master may thereupon, in his discretion, order such new evidence to be taken before the Standing Committee on Appeals. Ten days' notice of the time and place of taking such new evidence shall be given by said Committee to both parties and their counsel, and at such time and place either party may introduce any new and competent evidence.

68. No case shall be reversed upon appeal for mere matter of form, provided substantial justice shall have been done, and nc injury wrought by the informality or irregularity which shall appear.

69. After a due investigation of the case the Grand Lodge may by a majority vote,

1. Affirm the decision appealed from.
2. Reverse the decision.
3. Modify or change the decision.
4. Award a new trial.

70. If the decision, from which the appeal was taken, be affirmed, the Masonic standing of the accused shall remain as fixed by the decision of the subordinate tribunal.

71. If a new trial be awarded, the standing of the accused shall be, in the mean time, that of a Mason under charges, and as though no trial had been had.

72. From the taking of an appeal until its determination by the Grand Lodge, the standing of the accused (if he were suspended or expelled) shall be that of a Mason under charges: Provided, that he shall be debarred, during said time, from sitting in any Lodge.

NEW TRIALS.

73. A new trial in the Lodge shall proceed (unless special order be made to the contrary by the Grand Lodge or the Grand Master) upon the charges and answer already on file, and shall begin at the introduction of the proofs; the powers of the Master as to amendments, appointments of Commissioners and counsel and all other matters, being the same as upon the original trial.

74. If, upon new trial, the accused be again convicted, he may again appeal to the Grand Lodge. No number of convictions or acquittals can exhaust the right of either party to appeal.

75. An accused party under sentence may apply to the Grand Master (in the *interim*) for a new trial, who, upon satisfactory reasons appearing, may order the same.

76. The Lodge may grant a new trial upon the application of either party, by a unanimous vote, but not otherwise. Upon new trial ordered by the Lodge, the like rules govern in all respects as when ordered by the Grand Lodge or the Grand Master.

RESTORATION.

77. A Mason under sentence of definite suspension is, by operation of law, restored, at the termination of the period for which he stood suspended, to all the rights and privileges from which he was suspended, without any action of the Lodge or of the accused. The termination of the sentence is the termination of the suspension.

78. One under sentence of expulsion, or of definite or indefinite suspension, may be restored by the Lodge upon his own petition, if the same shall appear to be just and proper.

79. The Lodge may restore a Mason under sentence of definite or indefinite suspension by a two-thirds vote; but one under sentence of expulsion shall only be restored by the unanimous vote of the Lodge wherein the sentence was passed. Restoration from expulsion shall be in all respects the same as the admission of a profane, except as to the conferring of degrees.

80. Restoration shall not be granted by the Grand Lodge in any case, except from its own sentence; Provided, that this provision shall not apply to appeals, nor to persons expelled by Lodges which subsequently shall have ceased to exist.

GRAND LODGE TRIALS.

81. Charges against a Lodge or a Master shall only be preferred to the Grand Lodge.

82. The charges shall be in writing, and shall be filed with the Grand Secretary. The Grand Master shall thereupon issue a summons to the accused, commanding appearance at a time and place therein to be prescribed.

83. The Grand Secretary shall forthwith serve the summons, accompanied by an interlocutory order of the Grand Master, and a certified copy of the charges upon the accused, or cause the same to be done; which service shall be under the like rules as service of summons and charges in trials in the Lodge.

84. Upon the filing of the charges the Grand Master may make such order as the case shall demand. If the charges be against a Lodge, he may arrest its charter until the conclusion of the trial; if against a Master he may suspend the accused from office for a like period.

85. Trial in the Grand Lodge shall be conducted substantially under the same rules as a trial in the Lodge; Provided, that all judicial action in the Grand Lodge shall be taken by a majority vote, which vote shall be taken as the Grand Master may direct, and may be reconsidered at any time within twenty-four hours.

86. The Grand Lodge may punish individual offenders by the infliction of any of the Masonic penalties. A Lodge shall be punished by the arresting or revoking of its charter.

87. The Grand Lodge may, for sufficient cause, grant a new trial within its own body. If the Grand Lodge be not in session, the application for new trial shall be made to the Grand Master, who has, in the *interim*, power to grant the same.

88. The granting of a new trial in the Grand Lodge is attended with the like effects, as to the former decision or sentence and the Masonic standing of the accused, as in the like case in the Lodge, and the new trial shall proceed upon the same general principles as in the first instance.

BLANK FORMS.

[Grand Lodge has not adopted or prescribed Forms to be used in Masonic Trials; but it has *approved* the able work of R. W. Bro. H. M. Look, Grand Lecturer, entitled "MASONIC TRIALS."

All Lodges and Brethren, who wish to be guided by carefully prepared Forms, in the various phases and stages of Masonic Trials, are referred to Bro. Look's Digest of the Law of Trials, in which they will find all the forms needed.

These Forms may be found in that work under the following heads, viz.: CHARGES AND SPECIFICATIONS; SUMMONS TO ACCUSED; CERTIFICATE OF SERVICE; ANSWER; PROOFS; APPOINTMENT OF COMMISSIONERS; SUMMONS OF WITNESS; REPORT OF COMMISSIONERS; NOTICE OF JUDGMENT OR SENTENCE; NOTICE OF APPEAL; FORM OF APPEAL; ANSWER TO APPEAL; PETITION FOR RESTORATION; and APPLICATION FOR NEW TRIAL.

FOSTER PRATT,

Grand Secretary.]

ACT OF INCORPORATION

AND

CORPORATE BY-LAWS.

OF THE

GRAND LODGE, F. and A. M.

OF THE

STATE OF MICHIGAN.

ACT OF INCORPORATION.

(Session Laws of 1871, vol. 3, page 49.)

AN ACT to amend sections one, two, four and five, of act number two hundred and thirty-five of the Session Laws of 1849, relative to the incorporation of the Grand Lodge of Free and Accepted Masons of Michigan, and to repeal Act number sixty-nine of the Session Laws of 1869.

SECTION 1. *The People of the State of Michigan Enact,* That sections one, two, four and five, of an act entitled "An Act to incorporate the Grand Lodge of Free and Accepted Masons of the State of Michigan," approved April 2, 1849, be amended so as to read as follows:

SEC. 1. The Grand Lodge of Free and Accepted Masons of the State of Michigan, by that name and style are hereby incorporated, and declared a body politic and corporate in deed and law, with succession, and shall be in law capable of sueing and being sued, pleading and being impleaded, answering and being answered, defending and being defended, in all courts and places whatsoever, in all manner of actions, suits, complaints, matters and causes whatsoever, and that they and their successors shall have a common seal, and may change and alter the same at their pleasure.

SEC. 2. The officers of said corporation shall be the Grand Master, Deputy Grand Master, Senior Grand Warden, Junior Grand Warden, Grand Treasurer and Grand Secretary, for the time being, and they shall constitute the Board of Directors of said corporation, for the transaction of all business authorized by this act.

SEC. 3. This act shall be subject to the provisions of chapter fifty-five of the Revised Statutes of 1846, so far as the same may be applicable. (See Laws of 1849, p. 314.)

SEC. 4. Said corporation may make, under direction of the Grand Lodge, when assembled, and establish all By-Laws and Rules for its governance, and the governance of all subordinate Lodges under the jurisdiction of the Grand Lodge, relating to the business and property authorized to be done, held and conveyed by this act; and said corporation may take, hold and convey, as may be required from time to time, any real or personal estate for the purposes of their organization, and not at any time exceeding of personal estate fifty thousand dollars, and of real estate five hundred thousand dollars; and all real and personal estate so held may be conveyed by deed or bill of sale in the name of the corporation, executed by the Grand Master for the time being, and in case of real estate acknowledged by him to be the act and deed of the corporation, or by such other person as the Board of Directors may appoint for that purpose, with the seal of the Grand Lodge attached, and such conveyance so executed shall be valid and binding for all intents and purposes whatsoever.

SEC 5. Said corporation may hold real and personal estate of subordinate Lodges, in trust for the use of such subordinate Lodges, and do all acts and things in law relating thereto as trustees, and may convey the same as above, under the direction of such subordinate Lodges, and the Rules, Regulations and By-Laws of the Grand Lodge in relation thereto.

SECTION 2. Act number sixty-nine, of the Session Laws of 1869, is hereby repealed.

Approved March 15th, 1871.

CORPORATE BY-LAWS.

1. The Constitution and By-Laws of the M. W. Grand Lodge of Free and Accepted Masons of the State of Michigan, as heretofore enacted, are hereby established as the Constitution and By-Laws of this corporate body, in addition to which, for the better accomplishment and security of the objects and interests of the said Grand Lodge in its corporate capacity, this and the following By-Laws are hereby enacted.

2. This Grand Lodge hereby accepts all conveyances in trust of real or personal estate that have been heretofore executed by any subordinate Lodge or Lodges to this Grand Lodge, and pledges itself to accept any trust that shall hereafter be so executed by any Lodge under its jurisdiction, solemnly binding itself to faithfully keep, perform and execute any and all such trusts for the use and benefit of the respective beneficiaries, according to the terms and intent of the several conveyances so made.

3. Whenever the Grand Lodge shall receive a conveyance of any property, real or personal, in trust for any subordinate Lodge, the Grand Master shall forthwith execute and deliver to the Lodge for whose use and benefit such property shall be held, a declaration of trust pursuant to the form annexed to these By-Laws, under the seal of the Grand Lodge, and attested by the Grand Secretary.

4. This Grand Lodge, by its Grand Master and under its seal, as provided by section four of its act of incorporation, shall convey any real or personal property held by it as trustee, at such time, to such person or persons, and for such consideration, as shall be requested by the subordinate Lodge for whose use and benefit such property shall be held, and shall pay over to such subordinate Lodge on demand all moneys received in consideration for the property so conveyed, or received upon any mortgage, bond, note, or other evidence of debt held for the use and benefit of such subordinate Lodge, less the actual costs of collection.

5. This Grand Lodge hereby authorizes the actual or acting Worshipful Master of any constituent Lodge, for whose benefit any property shall be held in trust by said Grand Lodge, to effect, in its name as Trustee and as its agent a good and safe insurance

upon such property, and in such amount (not exceeding three-fourths the cash value) as shall be requested by such constituent Lodge; *provided* the premiums for such insurance shall be paid by the subordinate Lodge for whose benefit such insurance is effected. Whenever any loss shall be recovered by the Grand Lodge upon any insurance so effected, the amount so recovered shall be paid over forthwith to the subordinate Lodge entitled to the same, less the actual cost of collection.

6. The forms hereunto annexed are made a part of these By-Laws, and shall be used, when practicable, in the transaction of all the business provided for in these By-Laws to which the same are applicable.

7. The Grand Secretary shall make a full record of all applications, conveyances, instruments and documents of every kind executed by or to the Grand Lodge in the transaction of the business provided for in these corporate By-Laws, in a book or books to be kept by him for that purpose, and he shall keep an accurate index and counter-index thereto; and said books shall always be open to the inspection of the officers of the Grand Lodge and the Masters and Wardens of subordidate Lodges.

8. All subordinate Lodges under the jurisdiction of this Grand Lodge, and all members of the same, are hereby expressly prohibited from forming incorporate Masonic bodies under the laws of Michigan.

9. These By-Laws may be amended at any regular annual communication of this Grand Lodge and then only.

FORMS.—NO. 1.

APPLICATION FOR INSURANCE.

HALL OF_______________ LODGE, NO____, F. & A. M.,
_____________________________, 18____

To the R. W. Grand Secretary of the Grand Lodge of Free and Accepted Masons of the State of Michigan:

The said Grand Lodge is hereby requested to effect a good and safe fire insurance upon the following described property to wit:

[Description.]

in the sum of_______________________dollars, the cash value of said property being____________________dollars, for the benefit of____________________Lodge, No____, F. & A. M.

Please report your doings to me, and draw upon this Lodge for amount of premiums.

{Seal of lodge}

A_______________ B_______________, W. M.

Attest:
C_______________ D______________, Secretary.

[The preceding Blank is now useless by reason of the amendment of Corporate By-Law No. 5. The Master of each Lodge has the power to insure the property of his Lodge, in the name of the Grand Lodge.—G. S.]

NO. 2.

APPLICATION FOR CONVEYANCE.

HALL OF__________________ LODGE, No. ____, F. & A. M.,
___________________________, 18____

To the R. W. Grand Secretary of the Grand Lodge of Free and Accepted Masons of the State of Michigan:

The said Grand Lodge is hereby requested to convey to___________________ of__________________, the following described property, to wit:

[Description.]

for the consideration of___________________ dollars, to be paid as follows, viz.:

[Terms of Payment.]

the grantee to have the right of possession from and after___________________

Please make immediate report to me of the doings of said Grand Lodge in the premises.

{Seal of lodge}

A_______________ B_______________, W. M.

Attest:
C_______________ D______________, Secretary.

NO. 3.

BILL OF SALE TO GRAND LODGE.

KNOW all men by these Presents, that___________________________________of ________________________________Michigan, party of the first part, for and in consideration of the sum of one dollar, lawful money of the United States, to __________, in hand paid by the Grand Lodge of Free and Accepted Masons of the State of Michigan, in trust for________________ Lodge, No. ____, of Free and Accepted Masons, located at__________________, Michigan, party of the second part, the receipt whereof is hereby acknowledged, have bargained, sold, and by these presents do grant, sell and convey unto the said party of the second part, its successors and assigns, all the following mentioned property, to wit.:

[Description.]

To have and to hold the same unto the said party of the second part, its successors and assigns forever, in trust for the sole use, benefit and behoof of ---------------------- Lodge, No. ----, of Free and Accepted Masons, located at --------------------, in the State of Michigan, and to do all things relating to said property as trustee, and to convey, lease or insure the same under the direction of said ---------------- Lodge, No. ----, and the Rules, Regulations and By-Laws of the said Grand Lodge relative thereto.

And the party of the first part, for ---- heirs, executors, administrators and assigns, for the consideration aforesaid, doth covenant and agree to, and with the party of the second part, that the party of the first part, at the date and signing of these presents, is possessed of a full, perfect and unincumbered title in and to all of the said property, with full right to sell and convey the same, and that ---- will warrant and defend the title of the same to the said party of the second part, its successors and assigns, against all and every person or persons whomsoever.

In witness whereof------have hereunto set------ hand-- and seal this----- day of----------------, 18----

---------------------------[SEAL.]
---------------------------[SEAL.]

NO. 4.

DEED TO GRAND LODGE.

This indenture, made this---------- day of---------- in the year of our Lord one thousand eight hundred and ------------, between------------ of the first part, and the Grand Lodge of Free and Accepted Masons, of the State of Michigan, in trust for ---- Lodge, No. --, of Free and Accepted Masons located at--------, in the State of Michigan, of the second part, Witnesseth, that the said part-- of the first part, for and in consideration of the sum of one dollar in hand paid by the said party of the second part, the receipt whereof is hereby confessed and acknowledged, do- by these presents, grant, bargain, sell, remise, release, alien and confirm unto the said party of the second part, and to its successors and assigns forever.

[Description.]

Together with all and singular the hereditments and appurtenances thereunto belonging, or in anywise appertaining, in trust for the sole use and benefit of--------- Lodge, No. ----, of Free and Accepted Masons, now located at---------, Michigan, and to do all things relating to said property as trustee, and to convey, lease or insure the same under the direction of said---------- Lodge, No. ----, and the Rules, Regulations and By-Laws of the said Grand Lodge relative thereto. To have and to hold the said premises as above described, with the appurtenances, unto the said party of the second part, and to its successors and assigns forever. And the said part-- of the first part ---- heirs, executors and administrators ---- do-- covenant, grant, bargain and agree to and with the said party of the second part, its successors and assigns, that at the time of the ensealing and delivery of these presents,

____________ well seized of the above granted premises in Fee Simple. That they are free from all incumbrances whatever; and that ____ will, and ____ heirs, executors and administrators, ____ shall warrant and defend the same against all lawful claims whatsoever.

In witness whereof, the said part__ of the first part ha__ hereunto set ____ hand__ and seal__ the day and year first above written.

Signed, sealed and delivered in presence of

________________________[SEAL.]

________________________[SEAL.]

ACKNOWLEDGMENT.

STATE OF MICHIGAN, }
County of ____________ ________ } SS.

On this ______________ day of ________________, one thousand eight hundred and ________, before me, a ___________________ in and for said county, personally came the above named ________________________, known to me to be the person who executed the foregoing instrument, and acknowledged the same to be ______ free act and deed.

____

NO. 5.

DECLARATION OF TRUST BY GRAND LODGE.

Know all men by these presents, that the Grand Lodge of Free and Accepted Masons of the State of Michigan doth hereby declare and acknowledge itself to be in possession of all the following mentioned and described property, to wit:

[Description.]

by virtue of a conveyance by, (Bill of Sale or Deed) from__________ to the said Grand Lodge, dated the __________ day of __________ 18____, which said property is to be held in trust by the said Grand Lodge for the sole and only use, profit, benefit and behoof of______ Lodge, No. __, of Free and Accepted Masons, now located at ______________, in the State of Michigan, the same having been purchased with the money of the said ______________ Lodge, No. ____, and the said Grand Lodge, in consideration of the sum of one dollar paid by the said ______________ Lodge, No. ____, doth hereby covenant and agree with the said ______________ Lodge, No. ____, that the said Grand Lodge and its successors will faithfully discharge and execute said trust, and will at any time hereafter, when requested by said ______________ Lodge, No. ____, through the Worshipful Master and Secretary thereof, convey or transfer, lease or insure, said property, or any part thereof, as the said Lodge shall direct.

Witness the signature of the Grand Master and the seal of said Grand Lodge this ____________ day of ______________, 18____

{ Seal of the Grand Lodge. }

E____________ F____________, Grand Master.

Attest: G____________ H____________, Grand Secretary.

NO. 6.

LEASE TO GRAND LODGE.

It is hereby agreed, between ---------- part-- of the first part, and the Grand Lodge of Free and Accepted Masons of the State of Michigan, in trust for ---------------- Lodge, No. ----, of Free and Accepted Masons, located at ---------------, Michigan, party of the second part, as follows: The said ----- in consideration of the rents and covenants herein specified, do-- hereby let and lease to the said party of the second part:

[Description.]

for the term of ---- ------ from and after the ---- on the terms and conditions hereinafter mentioned, to be occupied for a Masonic Hail by ---------------- Lodge, No. ----, of Free and Accepted Masons; *Provided*, that in case any rent shall be due and unpaid, or if default shall be made in any of the covenants herein contained, then it shall be lawful for the said part-- of the first part ------ certain attorney, heirs, representatives and assigns, to re-enter into and re-possess the said premises, and the said party of the second part, and each and every other occupant, to remove and put out.

And the said party of the second part doth hereby hire the said premises for the term of ---- ---- as above mentioned, and doth covenant and promise to pay to the said part-- of the first part, representatives and assigns:

[Terms of Payment.]

It is hereby mutally agreed that the said Grand Lodge shall in no case be liable for rent or repairs beyond the amount of funds placed in its hands by said -------------- Lodge, No. -----. for that purpose. And also, that said Grand Lodge will, at its own expense, during the continuance of this lease, keep the said premises, and every part thereof, in as good repair, and at the expiration of the term, yield and deliver up the same in like condition as when taken, reasonable use and wear thereof and damage by the elements excepted, under the limitation aforesaid.

And the said part-- of the first part do-- covenant that the said party of the second part, on paying the aforesaid installments and performing all the covenants aforesaid, shall and may peaceably and quietly have, hold and enjoy the said demised premises for the term aforesaid.

The covenants, conditions and agreements, made and entered into by the several parties hereto, are declared binding on their respective heirs, representatives and assigns.

Witness our hands and seals, this -------------- day of --------------, 18----

------------------------------[SEAL.]
------------------------------[SEAL.]

ANALYTICAL INDEX

OF THE GRAND LODGE

CONSTITUTION, REGULATIONS AND BY-LAWS.

ABBREVIATIONS USED: G. L., Grand Lodge.—L., Lodge or Lodges.—Con. Constitution—O., Officer or Officers.—J., Jurisdiction.—G. J., Grand Jurisdiction.—M., Master.—G. M., Grand Master.—S., Secretary.—G. S., Grand Secretary.—T., Treasurer.—G. T., Grand Treasurer.—Com., Committee or Communication.

D

GENERAL INDEX.

www.ingramcontent.com/pod-product-compliance
Lightning Source LLC
LaVergne TN
LVHW021421110826
845150LV00007B/2022

* 9 7 8 1 4 2 5 5 0 8 9 2 0 *